ALWAYS RIGHT

Selected Writings of Midge Decter

Edited, with an introduction, by
Phillip N. Truluck

The
Heritage Foundation

Published by
The Heritage Foundation
214 Massachusetts Avenue, NE
Washington, DC 20002–4999
800-544-4843
www.heritage.org

ISBN 0-89195-108-3

Cover design by Brian S. Cobb

Table of Contents

Acknowledgments

This book has been a labor of love for me, and I am grateful to the Heritage colleagues who helped me put it together.

Special thanks go to Jean Barry, my assistant, who gathered Midge's speeches, pictures, and lore, and helped me in many ways to bring this project to fruition.

Thanks also to Dave Thomasson and Richard Odermatt for contributing their writing and editorial skills.

I would also like to thank Michelle Smith and Brian Cobb for the attractive layout and cover design.

Finally, my thanks to Midge for giving us so much to think about and for allowing us to pull together this wonderful collection of her work.

P.N.T.

Introduction

Twenty-five centuries ago, Socrates showed by his own example that a first-rate thinker is a first-rate pain—at least to those who are exasperated by clear minds and plain-spoken truth. Given the shortage of ancient Greek gadflies on today's politically correct landscape, it's a blessing that Midge Decter is keeping the tradition alive. Through much of the 20th century and steaming at full velocity into the 21st, she has wielded the eternal verities of human nature against a wide assortment of blights on contemporary life, and in the process brought agony to two groups that are particularly wrong-headed and dangerous: Communists and feminists. She finished off the Communists around 1990 and is well on her way to bringing down feminism.

It would be a mistake, however, to write Midge off as a contrary troublemaker. A troublemaker, no doubt. But contrary, no way. She is *for* freedom, and therefore against totalitarianism; *for* marriage and family, and therefore against feminism. True, she delights in breaking eggs (probably even more than we delight in watching her perform that operation), but her eye is always on the omelet. Anyone can express opinions about Communism or feminism or anything else under the sun, of course, and most people do. But what is it about those rare individuals like Midge whose thoughts are not only worth reflecting on but also worth setting down in durable print? I think there are at least three things that separate such minds from the common run: They take ideas seriously, they are *morally* committed to defending ideas that are indispensable to civilization, and their writing bubbles with a wit that draws its energy from a joyous sense of life.

Anyone committed to defend must be willing to fight, and Midge was one of the great though insufficiently appreciated fighters in the late war against Soviet Communism. That war, like most wars, was fought secondarily as one military power against another, but primarily as one philosophy against another, and it was on that ground that Midge earned her ribbons. Her moment of enlistment came, symbolically speaking, one morning in 1979. She was employed as an editor at Basic Books at the time, and Basic had just published a book called *The Romance of American Communism,* by Vivian Gornick. It was a collection of nostalgic and sentimental portraits of a bunch of American Commies. Midge recalls this moment in her delightful memoirs, *An Old Wife's Tale*:

> Now, if you work for a book publisher, you are supposed to pray for the success of all the books published by your publishing house; but on this particular morning when I opened the *New York Times* and discovered that its daily reviewer had slammed Miss Gornick's book, I cheered. Actually sat at the breakfast table sipping my coffee, and cheered. "How, after everything any reasonable person should have known by then about Communism, could we have put out such a book?" I shouted. And then: "A fine member of the house of Basic you are," I said; "you are clearly in the wrong business."

A year later she got into the right business, what she remembers as "my very own battle station, called the Committee for the Free World," which she established in New York. From her battle station, she stitched together a national coalition of intellectuals, authors, academics, and scientists who possessed the spine to stand unabashedly *for* capitalism and freedom, and *against* Communism and its totalitarian fashions. The value of her moral support for this coalition is easy to understate, because one of the left's favorite tactics is to make scapegoats and pariahs of anyone loyal to traditional American values, a loyalty that is especially intolerable in the world of letters.

Recall that the Committee was born at the dawn of the Reagan presidency, when standing tall against the Evil Empire was giving conniption fits to liberals accustomed to Jimmy Carter's soft-shelled *détente*. That stormy transition to sanity was supported by the Committee in many ways, not least through its monthly newsletters debunking the latest liberal lies and nonsense that were pumped through newspapers, magazines, and television documentaries. All told, the Committee claimed as many as ten thousand members in the United States and elsewhere, furnishing intellectual and financial ammunition.

But the battles extended beyond foreign policy and political philosophy. The 1960s had incubated an assortment of virulent ideas that, by the 1980s, had worked deep into the marrow of American culture. Few symptoms were more disturbing than feminism's fanatical, anti-family agenda, and it is here that Midge earned and continues to earn the respect and gratitude of levelheaded people. What she provides, in a nutshell, is a clarification and *validation* of common sense. You've probably found yourself in a social setting where someone is spouting the current feminist humbug. But you politely stifle the thought of how ridiculous they sound, because merely framing the words in your mind would give you the sort of countenance you would wear if you suddenly encountered a person with two heads.

Midge possesses the brains and courage to point out dangerous nonsense and call it by its right name, as you will see in the pages ahead. Among many examples is her discussion of a photo that ran on the front page of the *New York Post* at the beginning of the Gulf War. It showed a woman in full combat gear giving a farewell kiss to her infant cradled in the father's arms. As the riddle goes, What's wrong with this picture? No doubt many who saw it felt (at most) a vague stirring inside that something was amiss. But they look at the photo and move on because, of course, here is a woman who has achieved equal status with men and is joining them in the valiant defense of her country.

Of *course*? Count on Midge to stand up and state emphatically: Of course *not*!

> [Y]ou cannot tell—or rather, you are not supposed to be able to tell—the mommy from the daddy. The child, of course, knows who is what. No baby or little kid who is hungry or frightened or hurting ever calls for his daddy in the middle of the night. He might get his daddy, but it is unlikely that that would have been his desire.

> Everybody has always known such things:
> What is a husband; what is a wife? What is a
> mother; what is a father? How have we come
> to the place where they are open for debate?

Midge will tell you how we came to that place, and the clarity of her answer is one of many reasons why these speeches and essays were worth collecting and setting down in durable print. I am especially proud that they run here under the imprint of The Heritage Foundation. All were first published in Heritage publications or delivered at Heritage events. Midge has served on our Board of Trustees since 1981. How she came to that post provides yet another insight into her intellectual honesty.

She wasn't always a conservative. A few quibblers might say she isn't one now, but rather a *neo*conservative. That prefix, however, doesn't connote where she stands philosophically, but merely what propelled her there. As Irving Kristol famously put it, "A neoconservative is a liberal who has been mugged by reality." Midge was mugged during the sixties while hanging around *Commentary* magazine— co-mugged, more precisely, along with a young writer named Norman Podhoretz, who had courted and married her.

The sixties were a decisive decade for the couple. As she faithfully recalls in her memoirs, she and Norman "had grown more and more disgusted by, and contemptuous of, both the heedless and mindless leftist politics and intellectual and artistic nihilism of fashionable literary-intellectual society." She and other neocons found themselves in a narrow niche to the right of the Democratic party and to the left of the Republican party, and the niche was closing in on them. Most of this group, she remembers, "when the time came would fly into the arms of Ronald Reagan. From there it would be only a short and easy journey into full-blown conservatism."

Fly into his arms she did, and soon afterward launched the Committee for the Free World. And then one day out of the blue, Ed Feulner, president of Heritage, invited her to lunch.

> To my astonishment he asked me if I would be willing to serve on his board of trustees, and perhaps somewhat to his astonishment I took no more than three seconds to say yes. I hadn't the faintest idea what a trustee of The Heritage Foundation was expected to be, or do, but I heard a voice speaking the sentence "You must always join the side you are on," and the voice I heard was my own.

Midge wondered whether the invitation was a gesture that reflected the tokenism of the times. Did we want her on our board because she was a woman? Or perhaps because she was a Jew? She later asked Ed Feulner about that, and he told her he wanted to "make a statement," to show that the conservative movement was a big tent. "The problem was," she recalls, "that I could hardly be of service in enlarging the conservative tent because every time I met one of the leaders of the old-time conservatism, I discovered that we were in total agreement about everything that mattered."

Thus did a liberal of the 1950s become a conservative of the 1980s, unflinchingly facing intellectual errors and correcting them by assimilating ideas from the right. Always right. It takes uncommon intellectual courage to undergo such changes, and that is one reason to admire Midge Decter.

You will find many others in the pages ahead. As you read these conservative commentaries from her first-rate mind, you will understand why she is a first-rate pain to her opponents on the left. A few of them would probably be happy to serve her from the same cup of hemlock that did for poor Socrates. For our part at The Heritage Foundation, we raise a cup of cheer and wish her many more years of (in her serviceable phrase) "raising hell with the world."

Phillip N. Truluck
Executive Vice President
The Heritage Foundation

1 | Benign Victimization

Despite the fact that the policy known euphemistically as "affirmative action" is held in disfavor by an overriding majority of the American people, it seems safe to say that racial and sexual quotas are solidly established in our midst and will remain so for the foreseeable future. Indeed, nothing less than a serious social upheaval or major constitutional crisis—certainly no mere change of administrations or shift in the balance of congressional power—is apt to dislodge them. For public disapproval of the kind that can be expressed at the ballot box has not only proven to be no hindrance to the policy, it has in some sense provided reinforcement to the very process of its institutionalization. Affirmative action after all has a double agenda. First, there is the open agenda, the securing of places in society—preeminently in schools and jobs—for the members of particular groups claiming to have been intentionally and unjustly excluded in the past. And second, there is the somewhat more hidden one, which is to remove a certain order of social decision from the political arena and give it over to such agencies as the courts and bureaucracies where it can be kept securely out of public reach. Thus the widespread opposition to affirmative action has been held in the first instance to be itself prime evidence for both the justice and the necessity of the policy; and in the second instance has provided a spur to the policymakers to take matters ever more firmly into their own hands. Such a vicious circle will not easily be broken.

We can expect, therefore, to be living with quotas for some time—even though their most dedicated proponents hasten on every possible occasion to assure us that they are only a temporary expedient, a means of giving the provably disadvantaged that first indispensable leg up, after which reparation will have been made and justice achieved. By the time that golden age will have descended upon us, it is unlikely that any policy in a policy-ridden age will have done more than affirmative action to unsettle the series of delicate balances—between democracy and republic, individuals and pluralities, private rights and public necessities—it was once the unique political talent of this society to have struck.

Much has already been observed about the harmful impact of quotas on such instruments for maintaining the balances I have referred to as the schools and universities, the political parties, the agencies of government, and the economy. Moreover, that quotas are themselves indisputably unjust—not a means for doing away with the arbitrary exclusions of the past but merely a new form of arbitrary exclusion enforced against a new and different set of victims—has been frequently and forcefully pointed out (albeit as far as the courts are concerned, to no avail). It is on this point, as we have seen, that public opinion has drawn the firmest line: "unfair" is the characterization of quotas for which pollsters have found the highest level of assent. One issue, however (and it may be the most important issue of all) has so far not been paid the attention it deserves. That is the question of the impact of quotas on those who are their intended beneficiaries. How does preferential treatment affect those who are, in actuality or even only potentially, its recipients? Beyond this, how does it affect the feelings of others toward them? And finally, how does it affect the attitude of everyone toward the society he is living in?

There is, to be sure, good reason why this issue has been scanted. It resides in a realm difficult to get at directly, and in which the most important hypotheses are impossible to "prove." Attitudes are not opinions. Whereas opinions are held, and can be offered with varying degrees of forth-rightness by the holder, attitudes are more often than not *betrayed*—sometimes in very roundabout fashion and usually over a considerable passage of time. In addition, they do not, or let us say should not, openly enter into the construction of legal briefs, which has been the major forum of public argument about affirmative action. Yet the attitudinal, or psychic, or spiritual effect of this policy, both on individuals and on the nation as a whole, will undoubtedly prove to be the most lasting and by far the most destructive.

> Quotas are themselves indisputably unjust—not a means for doing away with the arbitrary exclusions of the past but merely a new form of arbitrary exclusion enforced against a new and different set of victims.

The Beneficiary Groups

The two main groups at whose behest quotas have been instituted and on whose behalf they have been administered are, of course, blacks and women. True, their ranks have been swelled by American Indians and that mysterious entity, "Spanish Surname," but these latter groups have imposed themselves primarily through an extension of logic (as other ethnic groups are lately and on the whole feebly attempting to do). It seems highly unlikely that they would have devised such a measure, or could have succeeded at having it implemented, in their own right.

Now, leaving aside the whole question of the respective merits of the claims of blacks and women to recompense for past injustice, the two are entirely dissimilar groups. Their linkage under the common heading of disadvantaged minorities is, literally, an incongruous one. Blacks have had a shared history; women as such have not. Blacks have had a shared cultural and political experience; women as such have not. In fact, women can hardly be said to be a "group" at all, as that term is generally understood. For historical reasons that remain to be properly explicated, however, the "causes" of women and blacks came to be treated as one and dealt with in a single fashion. In examining the issue of attitude, we are consequently bound to find the two groups, with certain inevitable and interesting variations, in an ever more similar condition.

It would be impossible, as I have said, to test an idea about that condition with any degree of scientific authority, but a good deal of so-called soft evidence is all around us. And what this evidence points to is that recipients of preferential treatment tend to suffer from a serious, and no doubt in many cases permanent and irrecoverable, decline in self-respect. The advantages gained in this fashion appear to be bringing little sense of either private or public satisfaction but only more strident assertions of grievances yet to be redressed. If a certain number of places are secured in this industry or that university, a large number is stormily demanded. For an outsider to remark upon any improvement in the situation of the aggrieved is for him to call down upon his head heated accusations of heartlessness and bigotry.

This otherwise anomalous behavior on the part of the beneficiaries of preferential treatment is often laid to the phenomenon known as the revolution of rising expectations. That is, we are told that more jobs and special opportunities lead to greater rather than lessened unrest among the affected minorities, because they provide a glimpse precisely of what full justice might look like and thus feed an ever more impatient desire to attain it. But this explanation is less than satisfactory, because what needs to be accounted for are not only the demands themselves but the increasingly sullen, surly, and bitter tone in which they are proffered. The tone is one not of people impatient for more but rather of people who have discovered that their sought-for special privileges, being unearned and therefore feeling unmerited, are doing them, spiritually speaking, no good.

So it is, for example, that large numbers of women who have been carried into the academy have devoted their teaching and research to the field of Women's Studies, which is to say, to the perpetuation of the anger and hostility responsible for their being there. So it is that large numbers of blacks who have been—almost, as it were, forcibly—hurled up the professional ladder have elected to make a profession of being black. So it is that in both cases individual as well as collective endeavor is frequently conducted with the kind of routine incivility that comes with the lack of a sense of self-worth. It is an open secret in this country, alluded to only in whispers but commonly recognized all the same, that students admitted to colleges and professional schools by virtue of helping to fulfill a racial or sexual quota tend quickly to feel defeated there. Even the qualified, insofar as they know themselves to have won a competition through the added benefits of a special allowance, sooner or later undergo crises which are crises of self-doubt. Nor for those employed can the nervousness and low expectations of employers, the all-too-evident and unavoidable response to a situation in which they have hired as they have in order to fend off lawsuits, union actions, and the like, contribute much to self-regard.

> Whatever people think about the justice or injustice of making special allowances for blacks and women, what they feel is that the objects of these allowances are somehow inferior.

How could all this be otherwise? At the heart of affirmative action, no matter how the policy is defined—whether as specific numerical quotas or only as desirable goals—lies the simple proposition that the individuals being hired or admitted or promoted would not in their own individual right be so. In terms of at least one of the central areas of their lives, in other words, they are not looked at or seen as individuals at all. In short, no matter how passionately affirmative action is sought and defended by its client groups, its underlying proposition is one that in the end must breed a painful resentment.

A Legacy of Resentment

But if self-doubt and resentment are the irresistible consequence of quotas for the beneficiaries, what can we imagine about the emotions of the rest of the people among whom they work and live? Polls, particularly the Sindlinger Poll undertaken for *Policy Review* (for which see the Spring 1980 issue), offer persuasive evidence that the opposition to affirmative action so widely found in the American public is not race- or sex-related. Plainly, people are against preferential treatment not because they are against blacks or women. Eighty-four percent of the people surveyed, to take an extremely significant example, answered No to the question of whether they would avoid dealing with black doctors or women lawyers. Their opposition is not to the groups but to the principle. But to repeat, opinions are not attitudes. In the daylight world where people actively and willfully make up their minds, Americans have undergone a massive diminution of racial prejudice. In the dark night of the soul, however, affirmative action itself is creating a new wave of racism and sexism. The new wave of racism and sexism differs from the earlier sort in that it is based not on fear, hatred, or guilt but on contempt. There is, of course, also a good deal of the kind of rage always engendered by the spectacle of unearned advantage, though in this case rage of this kind seems to be confined largely to the particular groups who are made to feel the immediate pinch on their own flesh— better qualified students who lose out in the competition with less qualified, white male academics, ethnics whose own minority status has been left out of consideration, and so on. On the whole, though, the more telling, and far more consequential, response is an involuntary, almost instinctive, inclination to patronize. Whatever people *think* about the justice or injustice of making special allowances for blacks and women, what they *feel* is that the objects of these allowances are somehow inferior.

Frequently, to be sure, this feeling is accurate. Affirmative action is not simply, and not even mainly, a legal or administrative arrangement; it is a frame of mind—a frame of mind best characterized by the term "double standard."

If someone must be included on whatever list in order to fulfill a quota or for the sake of appearances, a lowering of expectations and standards follows naturally. Such a lowering of standards extends far beyond jobs and school admissions. It seeps into the whole fabric of the culture. Accordingly, we have seen works written by blacks and women being praised all out of proportion to their merits, if any. We have seen public honors being bestowed for trivial if not laughable achievements. Perhaps more meaningful has been the application of a double standard to the public conduct of these groups: everything from lapses of taste to violations of the norms of decency to outright criminality has, under the sway of the general atmosphere of affirmative action, been condoned on the grounds that those who do such things are entitled by a history of inferiority to do no better. Just as the beneficiaries of affirmative action officially approve of the policy but necessarily feel demeaned by it, so the public at large may officially claim to feel no prejudice but cannot remain unaffected by the notion of group inferiority that is inherent in—indeed, that is the very determinant of—the double-standard system.

> Affirmative action is in its very inception based on a racist (and, in its subsequent application to women, a sexist) idea, which is that blacks, or women, given the removal of all barriers to opportunity, could not ever fairly compete.

Eighty-four percent of the people polled may believe that in principle they would experience no inclination to avoid, say, black doctors; in practice they are likely as time goes on to assume that in the absence of powerful evidence to the contrary, any black doctor is underqualified. Before long, the irony will have escaped no one: by means of a policy intended to shortcut past discriminatory practice the American populace will have become subject to a kind of prejudice which, if more subtle, is also by the same token infinitely more difficult to overcome. This prejudice, moreover, will be no unforeseen accident. Affirmative action is in its very inception based on a racist (and, in its subsequent application to women, a sexist) idea, which is that blacks, or women, given the removal of all barriers to opportunity, could not ever fairly compete. The rhetoric of the policy's supporters focuses not, as might be supposed, on equality but on incapacity. And in this rhetoric lurks the real underlying truth of attitude.

Equal Opportunity Overthrown

Finally, there is the problem of what affirmative action does to the attitude of everyone—those who benefit from it and those who do not—about the nature of the society in which he lives. The assault on the old idea that in America equality means equal opportunity has an impact on attitudes far wider than merely those toward race and sex. The message being daily hammered home by the arguments for a system of preferential treatment is, to put it bluntly, that society is a racket. There are no such things as standards of performance. Standards are a shibboleth; look how easily—with a stroke of the bureaucratic pen—they can be dispensed with. There is no such thing as achievement. Achievement is whatever the authorities in charge decree it to be. Above all, there is no such thing as justice. Justice is whatever happens to be dispensed by courts of law—malleable to current social conditions and fashioned to the humors of political and social convenience. To live in accordance with the belief that standards or achievements or justice have a reality that is to some extent objectively measurable, that they matter, and that they are worthy of aspiration is to be a sucker. All of these, too, are ideas difficult to resist in the dark night of the soul, no matter how earnestly or piously denied in the course of daylight inquiry.

A society cannot long remain vigorous and productive when so massive a cynicism about its principal beliefs is permitted to spread through the underground consciousness. A complaint frequently heard these days is that nothing works as efficiently as it used to, from telephones, banks, industrial products, all the way down to postage stamps. This is a serious charge against the United States, whose vitality is characteristically expressed in efficiency. No one has yet attempted—possibly no one has dared—to estimate the contribution of affirmative action to this decline. There is the direct contribution, in the form of the lowering of the standards of competence for employment in all sorts of areas. And there is the far more important indirect contribution made by the growing cynicism I have described: even those who are competent find it less and less compelling to take pride in what they do.

Here, then, we have the unmeasured, and in some sense unmeasurable, results of affirmative action. Blacks and women (and some few others) are learning in a new way to regard themselves of lesser account and being encouraged to hold themselves not accountable. Their fellow citizens are willy-nilly adopting a double standard toward them and being encouraged to pervert the sense of fair play into a virulent new strain of racism and sexism. The society as a whole is being undermined with respect to belief in the terms of its past achievements.

Difficult to weigh and measure with precision as these results may be, they are already being given unhappy expression in countless ways among us. If nothing intervenes to break the grip of this policy—and it is hard to see what will—they will be given countless more, and even unhappier ones, in years to come.

—Published in Policy Review, *Summer 1980.*

2 | The Intelligent Woman's Guide to Feminism

When the dust of this present age has settled, and our present turmoil becomes a subject for recollection in tranquility, let us imagine that some gifted young historian has set for himself the task of accounting for the attitudes and behavior of the affluent bourgeoisie in the fateful later decades of the twentieth century. Surely he will find (perhaps, in deference to my subject, I should say "he or she" will find) that not least among the puzzlements of the period is the passion with which a group of the freest, most vital and energetic—and most economically and physically privileged—young women in the history of the race rose up and proclaimed themselves to be the victims of intolerable oppression.

Perhaps even more puzzling in retrospect will have been the willingness of their contemporaries to affix to their uprising the name of feminism. For feminism properly understood is a view summed up in the simple proposition that women are the equals of men: that they are as intelligent, as competent, as brave, and above all, as morally responsible. It was this proposition, for example, that earlier in the century secured for women the right to vote, to educate themselves, to have and to spend their own money, and in general, to take upon themselves a share of the burden of civic responsibility. And yet easily the single most salient and unifying feature of the movement that erupted in the 1960s and that claimed to speak exclusively both to and for the problems of women—the movement that formally dubbed itself Women's Liberation—was its characterization of the condition of women as that of a pervasive and nearly universal inferiority. Despite any illusory appearances to the contrary, declared this movement, women everywhere were to be found mindless, helpless, cowering in the face of masculine power, their lives held in thrall to the whims and fashions of a manipulative culture. When their mothers, prior victims of male dominance, told them to marry, they married. When the needs and exigencies of a capitalist economy decreed that they must consume, they devoted their lives to a mad, spiraling round of consumption and to the breeding of a vast cohort of new consumers. When men, through the agency of a deceptive theory of mental health, sought a more plentiful supply of compliant sexual partners, women dutifully offered up their bodies in slavish service to something called the sexual revolution. And as for the less private side of life, when a contemptuous cultural and educational establishment sought to relegate them to professional non-achievement, they passively accepted the idea of their inherent incapacity to perform men's work. Thus nothing less than a complete overturning of all traditional social, sexual, and economic arrangements would suffice to bring women into a condition of full equality. The removal of all hindrances to this condition would not be enough. Women themselves must be altered, revolutionized. And with them, of course, men and the society that men have exclusively created.

This (to say the least) odd form of feminism fundamentally addressed itself to three areas of women's lives: to work, to marriage, and to motherhood. It also, naturally, addressed itself to the area of sex, but what it had to say on *that* entangled subject is very nearly literally unspeakable. For reasons of decency in public discussion, it need not detain us here—except to observe that in the end the movement has made the subject of sex almost indistinguishable from the medical practice of gynecology.

In each of these areas the movement provided an appropriate theory of women's victimization. In the realm of work, for instance, the main emblem of the status of women as an oppressed class was said to be the household. The age-old responsibility of women for the day-to-day physical well-being and welfare of the family, said the movement, had been the major means not only for keeping women away from all important sources of power in society but also for dulling their minds and souls into acquiescence with this state of affairs.

> Betty Friedan ...likened the condition of housewives to that of certain veterans of World War II who had suffered gunshot wounds to their brains.

In support of its theory, the movement embarked on a series of descriptions of the life of women at home unparalleled for their imagery of bleakness, depression, and unceasing, hopeless, thankless, fruitless toil since those nineteenth century reformist investigations of life in the workhouse.

In what might be taken as the founding document of Women's Liberation, Betty Friedan's *The Feminine Mystique,* the author likened the condition of housewives to that of certain veterans of World War II who had suffered gunshot wounds to their brains. Since one of Mrs. Friedan's more engaging habits as a public figure was the introduction of herself on innumerable important media occasions as the person graduated from Smith College with the highest grade average ever attained in that august institution, she herself had obviously escaped quite hand- ily from such a fate. Yet her account of the lot of the woman whose job was to run the house and look after the children was by no means the most lurid the movement was to produce.

That care for the household was a lot many women chose to have; that they deemed it important and, yes, rewarding; that they took pride in discharging its duties well; that it even afforded intermittent pleasure, was not— anyway, not invariably—denied by the movement. But the choice, the pride, even the pleasure—if such there should misguidedly be—were themselves only further evidence of how thoroughly, and how dismally, women themselves had assimilated the role imposed upon them by an oppres- sive society.

But if housework was the main emblem of women's inferior status, those who managed to evade it by pursuing careers were very little better off. For even in the office women were, with few exceptions, consigned to those tasks defined as "women's work." In addition to the despised secretaries—themselves hardly distinguishable from housewives in their obligation to be of service to others—even executives and qualified professional women were hopelessly identified with functions that were no more than extensions of the demand that women remain selfless, sympathetic, and attentive. That is, they tended to be social workers, nurses, schoolteachers, and therapists of various kinds.

It might, of course, have been asked, and specifically from a feminist point of view, whether the professions in which women tended to cluster and the work they tended to be drawn toward—called in tones and contexts of derision by Women's Lib the "helping professions"—did indeed enjoy lower status, or whether the movement itself held it to be inferior *because* it was work performed by women. Significantly, this question wasn't asked.

Whatever the answer, we have seen with what incredible rapidity the movement's constituents, under its goading, commenced in large numbers to enroll themselves in such formerly male-dominated professional schools as those in the law and medicine. (Would Women's Lib in the future say that once again they were doing what they were told? Might there one day come to be a derisive attitude toward the law, for instance, because so many women are now to be found there?)

I have left out one step in the process, by now so evidently well advanced, of creating a so-called new equality for women in the realm of work. For if, as was claimed, women had been denied equality of opportunity to take their place alongside men at the professional workplace, it was also claimed that they had also been denied the full development of their capacity to do so. The evidence was clear: women had not attempted and been denied admission to professional schools, or to executive training programs, or to candidacy for public office; they had not in any significant numbers applied for places in these precincts of power in the first place. Women were roughly 50 percent of the population. The only suitable test for the *true* achievement of equality, then, would be their ultimate ensconcement in half the positions of power, status, and wealth.

It would be pointless for their oppressors to argue that perhaps they had not *wanted* such power and prestige, that other ambitions and other values had in a majority of cases come first. Their very adherence to these other ambitions and values, such as a desire to marry and a disinclination to compete with the men they married, was a sign of how the culture had twisted and incapacitated them. By now they needed more than a change; they needed preferential placement.

> **Demand for affirmative action for women is the expression of less than complete confidence in women's capacity to compete up to the full extent that they wish to compete.**

This argument that society-bred fears and incapacities entitled those who suffered from them to a prior guarantee of places in schools and jobs to bring their number somewhat into line with their proportion of the population had, of course, already become familiar. It was the definition of justice and equality offered on behalf of the blacks by *their* equal rights movement. Its expression in terms of policy was affirmative action. Now, without going into a full discussion of the policy of affirmative action and the distress it is causing both to society as a whole and to the individuals said to be benefiting from it, one thing is quite clearly inherent in the logic of this policy and in the implicit thinking of its advocates: and that is, that it is the very opposite of an assertion of equality.

We may pass over as beneath comment the social and intellectual morality of the Women's Lib movement's equating the position of blacks with that of middle- and upper-middle class educated women in the United States. It nevertheless remains to be said that the demand for affirmative action for women is the expression of less than complete confidence in women's capacity to compete up to the full extent that they wish to compete, and, as such, bespeaks something considerably less than a firm feminist conviction.

A graphic illustration of Women's Lib's lack of confidence in its own claim (that but for a dominant sexist culture women would be equal to men in everything) is the proliferation, under its aegis, of a new women's literature. A visit to any newsstand or bookstore will make the point: women's magazines, magazines for working women, for professional women, for angry women, for chic women, abound. Moreover, in the section devoted to women's concerns that is now mandatory in every bookstore, one finds endless tomes devoted to women's medicine, women's psychology, women's novels, women's history, women's literary criticism—most of them comprising the reading list for movement-created and -administered programs of women's studies taught by affirmative action professors for the purpose of creating a comfortable ghetto for their female students. Consigning a young woman in university to the department of education or social work is as nothing (as a means of giving her the message that she dare not venture) compared with urging her to preoccupy herself with her own feminine experience and giving her college credit for it. Here again, the so-called new feminists have copied the blacks, and with much the same psychic effect: namely, an inner corroboration of the idea that they

Midge Decter

cannot be fitted into the world and the world must instead be fitted to them.

In the second area for which the movement has provided a theory of women's victimization, namely marriage, the theory is hardly less grim. Marriage, the movement has told its constituents, is merely an arrangement created by men for the provision of cheap labor and free sex. The contribution of women to that arrangement, therefore, is nothing more than a form of slavery or at best, indentured servitude. Marriage has been maintained by terror—the fear of actual male violence, the fear of being abandoned by one's husband without protection and without resources, and the fear of social contumely. Wherein, the philosophers of the new feminism have asked, does the married woman differ from the prostitute? Both, after all, exchange their services for money. Equality can only be established in marriage when that institution has been "redefined." ("Redefinition" is in general the movement's mystical, cabbalistic process for hastening the arrival, or the Second Coming, of the Messiah.) Thus husband and wife can only become equals in the movement's vision of equality when marriage has been redefined as a relationship in which there is no exchange. That is to say, in current fashionable parlance, when neither party to the marriage has a separate distinguishable role to play in the life of the other.

Translated into plain English, what this boils down to is that the only kind of marriage not demeaning to women is one in which the woman, too, will be entitled to have a wife—without at the same time having to be a husband. But with very few exceptions, women *wish* to marry and to be wives, sooner or later—and if there is any doubt on

20

this point, look around you—so if this notion of marriage is in force, women are left with the sense that to behave in a womanly way toward their husbands is to suffer only humiliation.

The result in the real world has been the far from edifying spectacle of marriages that have become a form of bookkeeping: What have you done for me today, and does it constitute a full and exact equivalent for what I did for you yesterday? A marriage without roles, as anyone who has witnessed the phenomenon at close range knows, has become not a mutual recognition of the equal importance to the enterprise of what both partners to it contribute—but a court of litigation. With respect to the issue of feminism in particular, it means that the feminine function in marriage is to be avoided by both husband and wife—or, since in actual life it can't be avoided, is to be regarded by both partners as only a collection of nasty chores to be got out of the way with as much dispatch as possible. Aside from what this has done to actual marriages—namely injected pure poison into them—it hardly conduces to respect for the womanly, either on the part of women themselves or on the part of the men with whom they live. By any meaningful reading of the term, this is a strange form of feminism. Indeed, ironically—or not so ironically— it has done a great deal to introduce and exacerbate the very conditions it claims to be responding to, that is, male violence and abandonment.

> Marriage, the movement has told its constituents, is merely an arrangement created by men for the provision of cheap labor and free sex.

One of the consequences of Women's Liberation, and in particular of the hostility toward men it engenders, is that it has relieved men of the responsibility for being proper husbands and fathers. That is why from the very first we have witnessed the otherwise astonishing phenomenon of women insisting upon the most terrible untruths about men and of men offering not one word of reply. When it was said to and about middle class American women that their husbands beat them, cow them, and kick them around (although, as everybody knows, what really goes on in the households of the educated middle class is quite opposite), not a single man stood up to say: "Wait just a moment, I have been working hard and under considerable stress to support my wife and family. Is that a just thing to say about me? I have tried to be decent and responsible, and *this* is the thanks I get?"

If women were refusing to accept the burden of womanliness, they were providing men with a perfect opportunity to be rid of the burden of manliness.

But there was no male resistance whatever to the indictments of Women's Liberation. This otherwise inexplicable passivity can only be understood in terms of the movement's pernicious appeal to the apparent short-term interest of men. If women were refusing to accept the burden of womanliness, they were providing men with a perfect opportunity to be rid of the burden of manliness. After all, manliness can also be called a burden as onerous as womanliness, if not more so.

So it is that more and more men are ceasing to be true husbands and fathers. Here we have the real consequence of the so-called role-less marriage. It is after all quite easy for a man to carry out the garbage and do the dishes and even wash the diapers. These are as nothing compared with the weight of being a real husband. Thus in the course of letting themselves off the hook of responsibility, women have also, of course, been letting men off that same hook. Thus wives *and* husbands are currently engaged in avoiding all the things they call onerous but that are in fact life-giving and health-giving.

Last but not least of the movement's theories about the lot of women is the theory of motherhood. Having to be a mother, as that "role" is traditionally "defined," says the movement, is the highest form of oppression of all. Women's Lib's pronouncements on the daily life of caring for children—on what it is like to spend time with them, look after them, and above all on the experience of the abiding, passionate, selfless attachment to them that motherhood entails—surpasses even its description of housework for bleakness and resentment. Babies are no more than a daily collection of soiled diapers. Toddlers are no more than daily imprisonment within four walls, or enchainment to a park bench. Schoolchildren are no more than a daily round of running exhausting errands—fetchings and carryings, mealtimes and quarrels. Above all, the passions and devotions of motherhood are no more than the imposition of the needs of the species on smothered and starving individuals. That children by themselves offer a considerable amount of meaning to life—I will not even mention pleasure—is a notion almost lost in the feverish mists of the new feminism.

Of all the ideas about the condition of women now circulating like the spores of an epidemic infection, the movement's theory of motherhood has, of course, taken least hold. Even for those intent on rejecting the idea that there is such a thing, a woman's nature simply will not be denied. Women continue to long for children, and continue to act on that longing. Even against considerable odds—even when marriage has become, on the whole, a light-minded undertaking, even in direst poverty, even in the face of a massive public campaign against their doing so, and even under those circumstances where men have been refusing in droves to stick around and be fathers—women continue to seek to be mothers. We see around us now, for instance, that cohort of women who have held out into their thirties, largely under the influence of the women's movement and related pressures, and who are now rushing around to get in under the deadline of what is called the biological clock. These women spent their twenties pursuing their careers (more often pursuing *themselves*) and, in *that* pursuit avoiding all commitment to the irrevocable. Now, some of them quite advanced in years, they feel the imperative of their unique nature as women and will not, whatever else happens to them, remain childless.

So the movement has lost on the score of this ultimate oppression, the oppression of motherhood, for which women will continue to volunteer. But the problem does not end there. In its teachings on the condition of women the movement has nevertheless sown the conviction that to live as women are destined, and thus privately compelled, to do—in no matter how attenuated a style—is to be consigned to inescapable inferiority. How many of the babies being born to this new cohort of mothers will be thrown into day-care centers—their contribution to meaning muffled, their pleasures lost—in order that their mothers may continue to deny any special virtue and value to womanliness? Heedless men and self-hating women have permitted this denial to go by the name of feminism, but it is in fact simply the hatred of women. In other words, the real sexism. For to call womanliness victimization is an expression of contempt for women more profound than any ever heard in the locker rooms, sales conventions, and executive suites of the old male-chauvinist world.

Why, then, have so many women embraced this peculiar assault on their value as women? The reason is that the movement, while it put them down, at the same time delivered a comforting message. It said to them: You are victims, and all your troubles and anxieties are the fault of somebody else. Women have indeed reached a new, if you will a revolutionary, condition. In the last fifty years, the combination of birth control, medical science, and modern technology have made it possible for them both to pursue careers and to have families. Now they are faced with an altogether new choice: Do I wish to have children or do I not wish to have children? This is both a new freedom and a tremendous new anxiety. The same is true with respect to the pursuit of careers. As any man could have told them—perhaps even tried now and then to tell them—that the pursuit of careers can be quite anxiety-ridden. In any case, women discovered, though some denied it, that they had taken on a whole new set of anxieties and fears.

> For to call womanliness victimization is an expression of contempt for women more profound than any ever heard in the locker rooms, sales conventions, and executive suites of the old male-chauvinist world.

In this situation, that is, facing genuine and unprecedented problems, women were confronted with a movement that sang to them a siren song: The reason that you are having difficulties, went this song, is that *they* have been conspiring against you. A true feminist movement under these circumstances would have said to women, in effect: Yes, indeed, life does have new difficulties; yes, indeed, it is full of new burdens and anxieties; yes, indeed, it is very hard. On the other hand, your new freedom can be very gratifying. You will need a lot of courage to secure its gratifications, but you *can* do so. Instead, they were told that their new freedom was the higher injustice. Any movement which offers an explanation for people's difficulties that has nothing whatever to do with them, and that requires no assumption of responsibility on their part, is bound to be very soothing. Witness the perversion of black pride and the undermining of black courage that has also resulted from just such a movement and just such a message.

> Any movement which offers an explanation for people's difficulties that has nothing whatever to do with them, and that requires no assumption of responsibility on their part, is bound to be very soothing.

If the movement had been addressing itself to the *real* difficulties of women, we should have seen an analysis of the condition of women today as one actually recognizes that condition to be. Such a movement would not have produced a literature which said that the educated American woman is a useless, helpless, brainwashed victim: for she is no such thing. If this movement had addressed itself to the problems of how much new will and courage it takes for her to deal with her new life as a person facing an altogether new kind of freedom, it would perhaps not have enjoyed such a wide response. But it would have been speaking truthfully, and it might in the long run have produced new vital juices instead of poison.

Our historian of the future, looking back, may describe, but will never be able to explain, any of this. The explanation does not lie in the domain of events and causes, economic conditions and social circumstances accessible to the historian's analysis. Nor can I pretend to offer it myself, except in the most vague and sketchy way. In the end, only a religious philosopher will be able to make our grandchildren, and their grandchildren, see how it was that women in our time came to be seized with such a loathing for what they ineluctably are. Perhaps he will say that it had to do with a refusal to accept the world and nature as God had constituted them. Perhaps he will say people—in this case, specifically middle-class, educated, Western women—were once blessed with a vast new accession of physical, social, and moral freedom, and sought desperately (let us hope he will have to say without success) to escape from it.

–*Published in* Policy Review, *Spring 1981.*

3 | Child Sacrifice

We Americans have many public disagreements, but privately it can be said that we are nowadays firmly bound together by a common unease. Something is going wrong with the constitution of our individual lives. Women, for instance, are noisily embattled, while men smolder in resentful silence. Drugs and alcoholism, untouched by years of effort to control them, remain at the top of the list of social menaces. Despite the wide availability of effective means of contraception, in some American cities abortions outnumber live births. A new psychotherapy or mood-altering chemical gets produced, as it seems, every minute. And, of course, there are all those divorces, all those lonely and self-seeking men and women hopping from marriage to marriage in search of what they cannot say, all those children abandoned by their fathers, and even, nowadays, abandoned by their mothers. We are forced to ask ourselves a question so vast and general as, what is going on with us? How is it that a people blessed by God, or if you will, fate, with better health, longer lives, greater comfort and personal freedom and economic well-being than any previous peoples in history, should give so much evidence of deep trouble?

Neither I nor anyone else can presume to answer this question in full. But I would, in the briefest way, like to suggest an area in which we might begin to find some understanding.

For a generation now, millions upon millions of Americans—I will not say all—have been engaging in child sacrifice. Less bloodily, perhaps, but no less obediently than certain ancient groups of idol worshippers, we have been offering up our children on the altar of a pitiless god. Nor do I mean this as a flowery metaphor. In our case, the idol to whom we have sacrificed our young is not made of wood or gold but of an idea. This idea, very crudely put, is that we are living in an altogether new world with not yet fully understood new moral rules. As inhabitants of this supposedly newly ordered world, we tell ourselves, we have no right to cling to or impose on others outmoded standards of behavior. On the contrary, everyone has a right, even an obligation, to make up his own rules—and with these rules, to make up his own preferred mode of living. This idea is no mere abstract proposition with us; we have translated it, socially, religiously, politically, and juridically, into the stuff of our everyday existence. And we have, as I said, literally sacrificed our children to it.

Not so very long ago a whole generation of this country's middle-class children rose up in late adolescence and said they could see no reason to prepare themselves to take on the burdens of adult life: to serve their country, for instance, or educate themselves, or make a living. They left school, they ran away, they drugged themselves; in milder cases, they just kind of hung around, growing pale, unkempt, unhealthy, and truculent. And untold numbers of them committed suicide. Again, I do not speak metaphorically. In 10 years the suicide rate of those from 18 to 25 increased by 25 percent. How did we respond to this, we elders—we parents, teachers, clergymen, journalists, civic leaders, and yes, legislators? We applauded them. We said they were the best generation ever seen, they were great idealists, far superior to ourselves. We said they had discovered a new way to live. In short, we abandoned them. Just as surely as if we had with our own hands bared their necks to the ritual knife, we sacrificed them on the altar of our own moral irresponsibility. Those who managed to save themselves did so with no help from any of the authorities in their lives, neither parental, religious, nor intellectual. For none of these authorities would tell them what they needed to know: that life is real and weighty and consequential; that life is good, and only good when it *is* real and weighty and consequential; that it requires discipline and courage and the assumption of responsibility for oneself and others, and that it repays, and *only* repays discipline and courage and the assumption of responsibility for oneself and others.

A whole generation of this country's middle-class children rose up ... and said they could see no reason to prepare themselves to take on the burdens of adult life.

Why did mothers and fathers, teachers and ministers, lawgivers and judges, why did all the figures on whom children depend to teach them how to live a decent and rewarding life refuse to tell them what they needed to know? Because they themselves had not the courage of any convictions. How many parents sent—still send—their adolescent children off, unaided and morally and psychically unprotected, into the treacherous ocean of sex simply because they have not the courage to say what they truly believe: that sex in childhood is a dangerous and debilitating and life-denying force? As a society, we do not even any longer have the moral courage to cast out in horror—a horror we all feel—the child pornographer, the pedophile, the committer of incest. We hem and haw and let the courts decide, which they usually do on the basis of fine points of legal procedure.

Does the First Amendment protect the exploiters of 7- and 8-year-old boys for pornographic films? Is that really one of the constitutional rights that have made this country a glory of freedom?

The truth is, we have lost the collective ability to make the simplest moral assertions. And if we have lost it collectively, we are surely in the process of losing it individually as well. For people precisely cannot make up their own lives. They are constituted to be members of communities. They cannot live themselves and cannot bring up their children, not for long, by a standard that finds no confirmation in the surrounding community. An individual's inner resolve, when it must be engaged every day in a battle against the surrounding moral atmosphere, begins to erode and crack. A community that does not love virtue—yes, I will dare to use so archaic a word—takes an unimaginable toll on the virtuous. Instead of rewarding, it punishes them. Out of historic error, out of sloth, out of cowardice, out of lack of collective will, we are permitting ourselves to become a society that punishes the virtuous. That punishment is every day being incorporated into the laws of the land, written and unwritten.

It is the family—the greatest tribute to and the most brilliant invention of the human moral capacity—that has lately taken the greatest punishment of all. For one thing, we pretend no longer to be sure what *is* a family. We debate publicly, as we did even at a White House conference not many years back: Is a family the same thing as a household? Is it two lesbians? Is it a man and a woman sharing the same roof out of wedlock? Why not? Are we not, after all, free as people living in a new order to make up our own definitions? In attempting to erase its uniqueness as an institution, we remove from the family the community affirmation that is the absolutely essential ingredient to its strength as an institution. It was claimed, and our policy makers concurred, that society engaged in unfair discrimination against those who chose (I believe the fashionable word is "opted") not to live in traditional families. But such discrimination, in everything from tax policy to public speech, is precisely the means by which a society makes known its standards and values. Why should a society that professes to believe in the family *not* discriminate in its favor? Even to have to speak of "belief" in the family, as if it were an alternative among many, is a sign of our pathology. Indeed, by turning the family into a merely voluntary, optional relationship, we have ironically increased its capacity to make its members unhappy. Thus our divorce rate.

The family, as I have said, is a brilliant moral invention. It teaches us that life is not lived alone. To be a parent is to discover, sometimes with considerable surprise, that there are lives more valuable to one than one's own. To be a child of parents is to experience two indispensably humanizing things. The first of these is that no matter who or what one turns out to be, there are two people, *one of each sex,* to whom one's existence is and will ever remain of overriding importance. The second is to incorporate into one's being the knowledge that human life, as opposed to animal existence, is a system of mutual obligations and dependencies.

To get beyond self is the only possibility for happiness, just as to understand obligation is the only possibility for genuine individual freedom. That may, as little children are wont to say, be "no fair," but it is the truth. Thus the family—as everyone knows, no matter how many revolutions of consciousness and being he claims have taken place—is a mother and a father and their children. And thus, too, the family is one of society's first priorities.

I do not pretend to have any simple answer as to how we can get ourselves out of our present moral morass. But I do know that it will be necessary for us to begin to talk to one another from the heart instead of out of a lot of junky and morally impertinent fashionable ideas. And I do know that it will be necessary for us as a society, without fear for the trendy opinion of mankind, forcefully and vocally to discriminate in favor of what we all, deep down, still long to believe is good and valuable and right.

—Published in Policy Review, *January 1984.*

4 | The U.N. and U.S. National Interests

The United Nations as an institution was an effort to sell American values, American political values, to the world. It was an invention of the United States, and one might say in admiration of this country—and also in despair for the quality known as American innocence—that only the United States *could* have invented such an institution as the United Nations. For it was an effort to offer to the world a model of the liberal parliamentary order. A parliament of nations. And unlike earlier parliaments of nations, this one, said its inventors, was going to be truly representative. Therefore it included a body, the General Assembly, which gave equal voice and equal representation to all the sovereign nations. This resulted in its being unable to reflect the realities of power in the world, which is undoubtedly one of the reasons why it has been unable to function really as a peacekeeping organization. I am not going to go through a taxing history, but what has become of this American liberal invention we know. It has been turned around 180 degrees into a center for the articulation and the legitimization of tyranny, in the names of "justice," "freedom," and all those other words which we contributed and which daily get perverted in that institution.

We find ourselves now in a peculiar predicament. We are not only the founding spirit behind this organization, we are its major funder. It sits, appropriately to its initial intention, in the city of New York, the symbol in this country of the uplifting of the formerly downtrodden (which was surely the impulse behind the creation of the institution), and the city that in this country best typifies that process. And yet its major role in the world now is to be the center for agitation against the values by which, and under which, it was created.

> The notion that the free nations of this world are to be lectured to and hectored and made demands of by some of the most tyrannical nations on earth in the name of justice, is a perversion of language.

The U.N. is a center of agitation against the democratic order, not to say American society, and certainly not to say American national interest. How have we gotten ourselves into this spot, where we are the host and the major funder of an institution most of whose deliberations, and particularly those to which the press and the public pay no attention, are inimical not only to our interests and not only to our survival but to the very things that we and this institution itself stand for? Well, we do not have to discuss now the process by which this happened. The question is, what should we do about it?

One of the ways we have allowed this process to happen under our very noses is that we have not taken the United Nations seriously. We have paid for it; we have genuflected before it; we have been unfailingly polite toward it. We have sent children out with little boxes every Halloween. But we have not taken it seriously. By not taking the U.N. seriously I mean we have not, certainly not as a nation, sufficiently attended to what was being said there, to what was being put into the documents of that institution. That we now have a Mission to the United Nations which *does* take it seriously in this way, which exercises the right of reply, which makes the argument, is unusual, possibly unique. But this cannot be counted on in the long political future because it very much depends on who is at the Mission. And it seems to me, I hope that my friends who are members of USUN will not misunderstand the spirit in which I say this, it seems to me somewhat like locking the barn door after the horse has been stolen. The damage has been done.

A major damage—and it is a major damage to a democratic society—has been the corruption of language. This is also a subject about which Ambassador Kirkpatrick feels very strongly. The corruption of language, the distortion of the word justice, even distributive justice, that lies behind the notion of the New International Economic Order, the New World Information Order—and who knows what other new world orders lie in store for us—the notion that the free nations of this world are to be lectured to and hectored and made demands of by some of the most tyrannical nations on earth in the name of justice, is a perversion of language and thought that we have permitted to happen and that has left us all in a state of deep and dangerous befuddlement. The result is it takes us ages simply to sort out a question before we can even begin to address ourselves to it. Having said this, I suppose it will not surprise you to hear me offer, with all the seriousness I can command, the proposition that it is possible that the course of peace and the course of justice, not only here but throughout the world, would be best served if the United States left the United Nations.

Of course, as Frank Shakespeare suggested about the salutary effect on UNESCO that Elliott Abrams had when he threatened it with a shaky future, merely proposing that the U.N. should leave New York City might exercise a great and salutary disciplinary influence on the delegates, and particularly on members of the secretariat to the United Nations, who get to live here all the time regardless of what happens in their governments.

The Heritage Foundation is putting out a series of papers telling us what has been going on in this institution with our passive collusion over the years: among other nice things, the support for terrorism and the house room given to Soviet intelligence agents. So I am not being frivolous, nor am I being a little old lady in tennis shoes, when I say to you that for the sake of international relations, as well as the sanity of American thought, we ought to confess our error to ourselves and get out. I know the argument is made that there is great value for us in remaining at the U.N. and talking to its delegations and continuing to conduct dialogue with them. But I think that genuine dialogue is impossible when people do not agree even on first principles and so I have come here today to propose that it is time for us to reconsider our membership in, which is to say, the future assured existence of, what has proven to be a ghastly institution,

> **The course of peace and the course of justice, not only here but throughout the world, would be best served if the United States left the United Nations.**

The best example of the linguistic corruption I referred to is the invention and dissemination and complete acceptance of something called "Third World." I submit that there is no such thing as the Third World, and I submit that all our pieties toward this non-existent construct have not conduced to the welfare of the people living in the countries that are supposed to be included in it. There is really no such category. What can you say about an idea that includes Taiwan and Uganda? What you can say about it is that it is an intellectual confusion and a linguistic perversion and that aside from what it has done to our capacity to think through our problems has undoubtedly contributed in immeasurable ways to the further immiseration of the world. This is not what we had in mind, and I think the time has come for us no longer to participate in the process.

*–Midge Decter participated in a
panel discussion with this title on June 1, 1982.*

5 | Is Conservatism Optimistic or Pessimistic?

A t first glance, the question of whether conservatism is optimistic or pessimistic seems to touch on an issue centrally important to the discussion of what it means to be conservative. We are all, I think, aware of the, lately mostly unspoken, debate out of which this question arises: it is a debate about nothing less critical in determining a person's political and social attitudes than his vision of the nature of man. We also know—or should—where conservatism comes out in this debate, that to be conservative is to view man as a deeply flawed and fallible creature, restricted in understanding, beset with temptations and base impulses, a sinner (or, I prefer to think of it, a cheater, whose entire history on earth has been one long series of stratagems to renege on God's bargain). A true conservative, then, believes that this imperfect and imperfectible creature, who must vacillate forever between singing with the angels and stampeding with the animals, needs laws and traditions and ordered expectations of life for the fulfillment of his moral, which is to say, his human, nature. In a good society, the conservative believes, these laws will be just and humane, these traditions ennobling, these ordered expectations properly anchored in piety. But in no society can they be dispensed with. In this, the true conservative differs fundamentally from the true libertarian.

"Yetzer ha-adam ra mi'neurav," God, whose first language in those days was Hebrew, says in the book of Genesis: "From the days of his youth the inclination of man is to evil." Having been granted free will, man can be counted on to spend a goodly portion of it on disobedience. The history of mankind since the days of the Creation I do not suppose has given God any compelling reason to change his mind. For conservatives, you might say it has been the better part of political wisdom to bear that divine discovery in mind and to incorporate it within their sense of political expectation.

Yet we see about us a conservative movement—active, busy, lively, and bursting with ambition to alter the world's social, political, and economic arrangements. Is there not some contradiction between a "movement," particularly a movement currently occupied with political action and the wielding of political power, and conservatism as it essentially is?

Just such a challenge to the conservative movement has lately been thrown out by more than one conservative thinker, and it is a challenge not to be lightly dismissed. Some of the conservative bustle around us does smack dangerously of liberalism, in the sense of suggesting or implying that there are policies, certain public "fixes," that may yet restore us to Eden. Paradise-to-come is after all the preserve of liberalism, whose founding belief that men, and by extension the society of men, may yet be brought to perfection has been known to lead—need I even say it—to massive tyranny, bloodshed, and brutality.

So yes, from a certain point of view conservatism does obligate its adherents to sustain, and remain mindful of, a firm bedrock of pessimism.

But having said that, I find I have said very little. Important as the question in my title seems when one first hears it, on further consideration the opposition of optimism and pessimism only leads us directly back to First Principles—a terrain where banalities and "big think" lie in wait for us at every turn.

Some of the conservative bustle around us does smack dangerously of liberalism, in the sense of suggesting or implying that there are policies, certain public "fixes," that may yet restore us to Eden.

Permit me, therefore, to ask, and attempt to answer, a related but very different question. My question is a simple one, and carries us into the realm of everyday experience. The question I prefer to ask today is, does conservatism make you gloomy or cheerful?

My perhaps paradoxical answer is that it is the very pessimism of conservatism which makes it the greatest possible source of good cheer for those who follow its dictates. For cheer is the wellhead of (actually it is the same as) vitality; and nothing is more conducive to the genuine flow of vitality than a full-hearted acceptance of the limits of man's nature and capacities.

My impulse at this point is simply to call to the witness stand a Mr. William F. Buckley, or a Dr. Edwin J. Feulner, or anyone of scores of figures, public and private, who may or may not be familiar to you, to call them to the stand, point my finger, and let my case rest. A cursory examination of just half an ordinary day in the life of either the gentlemen I have named or others I have not named would provide all that is needed by way of an ideal definition of vitality.

> Nothing is more conducive to the genuine flow of vitality than a full-hearted acceptance of the limits of man's nature and capacities.

Nevertheless I shall try, albeit gropingly, to put into words what I mean. By good cheer, I do not mean that conservatism is guaranteed to leave 'em dancing in the aisles. Each of us in this room has certainly had a fair share of days over the past few years colored by worry and frustration. One might almost be able to discover a perfect inverse ratio between the height of the hopes that overtook many conservatives upon the coming to power of Ronald Reagan and the intensity of their frustration at having to learn, or we might better say, relearn, that the world even as presided over by a man completely in tune with their ideas is made of pretty intractable stuff. (Here indeed was a case when a bit of distanced skepticism, that attractive and reliable first cousin of pessimism, would have stood more than a few of us in good stead.) Nor have our worry and frustration abated in the least with the passage of time. On the contrary. There are so many things we see so clearly—no doubt, being human, we have confusions of our own, but there are whole patches of clarity that constitute a consensus among us—and yet we must stand by and watch our countrymen being drowned in obfuscation and superstition; our President wavering uncertainly between antipodes of desire, the desire to do what he believes is necessary and the desire to be loved; and a whole flock of opposition politicians whose dream of returning to power has suborned their sense of responsibility to the nation. Beyond politics, we see cultural and spiritual catastrophes brewing. Our cultural and artistic institutions are a disgrace; our universities, an open scandal. Millions of our fellow citizens rush around adopting this phony nostrum and that, all the way from miracle diets and special exercises to the reorganization of work and family life, all in the name of their unconcealed longing to evade the reality both of the lives given to them and of the death that inevitably awaits them. In the process they are surrounding themselves, and us, with a culture so trivial and poverty-stricken, so mean and small and self-referring, as fairly to take the air right out of our lungs.

C onservatism makes you cheerful because in ways not always understood by many conservatives it tells you what it is given to you to do and what it is not given to you to do in the course of each passing day.

So the cheer I am talking about has nothing to do with the sensation of political and cultural success. For the conservative movement, as for any other, successes and failures—and the satisfactions and disappointments respectively proper to them—can be plotted on some curve that does not in its details necessarily provide a coherent picture. But that is quite beside the point. Conservatism makes you cheerful because in ways not always understood by many conservatives it tells you what it is given to you to do and what it is not given to you to do in the course of each passing day. And the true possibility for joy in one's undertakings lies not in their outcome but in the undertaking itself. Happiness, as Aristotle tried to teach us, is not a condition in itself, but the accompaniment of an activity.

Each of us, of course, translates these large but very specific truths about human existence into the terms most familiar to him. I am, as you know, a Jew, and for me the exemplary illustration of the point I am trying to make is contained in an old East European Jewish folk tale. For me, it is the quintessential conservative story, though its original author would undoubtedly have been bewildered to think that one day there would be a world in which it would seem necessary to give it such an adjective.

> To accept the knowledge that as a human being you are limited... as true conservatism requires, is to understand that life is not a right but a gift.

This is the story about a humble shoemaker, Mendel, from a muddy little village somewhere in the Jewish Pale of Settlement who dies and in due course arrives at the entrance to the Judgment Seat. In all too familiar a manner, he begins to apologize for his humble station in life and to offer various excuses for his not having been able to rise above it. The heavenly minions who are to usher him before his Final Judge interrupt him and say, "Listen, when you stand before the Creator, He will not ask you why you were not Moses or King David or one of the Prophets. He will ask you why you were not Mendel the shoemaker."

To accept the knowledge that as a human being you are limited—indeed, limited most of all in that you can never really know what those limits are and how far beyond your present capacity they extend—to accept this knowledge, as true conservatism requires, is to understand that life is not a right but a gift. There is no single life, however lousy, however full of pain and anxiety and seeming unfairness, that is not a gift. Gratitude for this gift, even if it seems to others to be a meager or worthless one, is the beginning, the middle, and the end of the attitude to which people would nowadays affix the rather paltry term "conservative." And everything you think about the most mundane and worldly matters preoccupying you these days—tax bills, for instance, or welfare policy, or what to do about Nicaragua—in the end hangs on that one underlying issue: whether to bless or curse whatever of life has been granted us. Atheists tend to think of religion—correction: like to think of religion—as dreary, because it is so full of "Thou shalt not's" and also "Thou shalt's" that are so difficult to live up to. But

We are not guaranteed victory, but we are guaranteed the chance to pursue it day by day.

most, perhaps all, of the world's great religions—I do not understand Buddhism and so will not speak for it—are systems for adumbrating ways of being grateful. Some emphasize this, some emphasize that, but each is based on the sense of miracle that we are here at all and on the understanding that we may not ultimately know, and are not to contend with, why. It you think this is not a recipe for cheer, try getting up in the morning and, before facing even the first of the day's problems, actually saying a word of thanks for the fact that you lived through the night.

The opportunity to grapple one's problems, if need be, to break one's head against them, is, conservatism understands, the only opportunity needed and the only opportunity granted. We are not guaranteed victory, but we are guaranteed the chance to pursue it day by day. What could be more enlivening?

As for the other side of my equation, that is, optimism and gloom, I ask you to consider. Suppose you believed that the history of world has been one long uphill progression from darkness to light, that man as we now know him is merely the capstone of this progress so far, and who knows what great permutation we may expect to come next. We can see what dreams such optimism is already driving people to. There is the dream that women need no longer be women, nor men, men. There is that dream that science and medical technology will, if only they stay at the task long enough, enable us to live forever.

There is the dream—or rather, it is a vast complex of interconnected dreams—that the right tricks of social organization will make it possible for everyone to be equally rich, equally admired, equally permitted to pursue his transient desires; that sex will be like the gentle rain, abundant, morally neutral, without consequence, physical or emotional, a cleansing and soothing exercise; that babies will be produced painlessly and reared flawlessly by some general entity called society; that no handicapped people or potential sufferers of dread diseases need be born to trouble our serenity and that handicaps or diseases created by accidents of fate can be cured or their bearers disposed of; that crime will be extirpated and violence expunged from the earth. There is the dream that one might call the dream of perfect communication, in which more highly evolved men, having somehow disposed of their troublesome inferiors, will sit down together and, understanding one another, put an end to war. All this—if only we are clever enough to figure out how to arrange it.

There are those who will say that I exaggerate and caricature the aspiration of the optimists. I do not. For every dream I have just listed, there is an abundant body of documents, published in books and read and celebrated in language of the deepest reverence by spokesmen for the liberal community.

As I said, suppose you believed such things: what would happen to you? First, of course, you would be able to put away all the hard and great books, those treasured storehouses of the accumulated experience and earned wisdom of our ancestors, those benighted children of darkness past. (In fact, many of the educational institutions dominated by the liberal, or optimistic, world view have to a large extent already done so.) Coming into the adult world, then, naked as a jaybird and with an equally naked and uncomprehended technology available to you for your manipulations, how would you feel? You would feel that you were owed a perfect, painless, conflict-free existence, and that therefore real life, which is none of these things, and cannot be, was a kind of unfair conspiracy against you. The equal riches and equal admiration that you took to be your due, to the extent that they actually did get more equal, would turn out to be equal poverty and equal contempt. Injured vanity, jealousy, the decline of your powers—no matter how many health regimens, faceless sexual encounters, and applications of new medical techniques you obediently took upon yourself—would still be with you, now experienced as injustice and failure.

It is not for nothing that "rage" has been one of the favorite words, offered in explanation of all deviant behavior, of the liberal community for something like a couple of decades now. The rage imputed to others is as likely as not some form of what the psychologists have termed projection. The rage so frequently invoked is more often than not the invoker's own. If you do not believe me, just look at the faces, listen to the voices, think about the

> The denial of real moral choices for the sake of unreal ones leads to inner starvation.

language used by those declaring their determination to gain dominion over, and remake, human nature. Try to comprehend what these optimists are really saying. You will find that they are not saying that we need to do as much as possible—possible—to improve the lot of the poor; they are saying that a life in poverty is not worth living. They are not saying that we must use the science God gave us to make the world hospitable to its expanding population; they are saying that we must use it to make sure that there will be fewer people, less life. They are not saying let us make ourselves worthy of the mysterious gift of being alive by cherishing our young, so that they may cherish their young; they are saying let us allow ourselves only those young who are easy to cherish so that they may be worthy of our cherishing. They do not say let us reason together about how to protect and defend the best political system we have yet been able to devise; they say, let us speak to one another only of its flaws that in so speaking we may encourage one another to hold out for the best system that has never yet been, and that may never yet be, devised. In other words, into their very optimism is built the refusal of the possible, and into such refusal is built eternal disappointment.

The habits of rage and disappointment, if you will permit me again to have recourse to the language of psychotherapy, lead to depression. Never mind that this particular kind of depression claims for itself the name of idealism. Idealism, even as it defines itself, is the denial of real moral choices for the sake of unreal ones. You all know the fable of the donkey on the road who sees a bale of hay in the field on either side of him and, unable to choose, starves to death. The denial of real moral choices for the sake of unreal ones leads to inner starvation.

There you have your social optimism: unweening ambition leading to rage, unholy fantasies leading to disappointment, and perverse will leading to spiritual starvation. With such hopes and such dreams, who needs poison?

A lot of ordinary Americans know these things in their bones. They do, it is true, like to hear about a shining city on a hill. They like to hear about it just because they have for so long been up to their necks in optimistic gloom. But what they settle for, and gladly, is a not-too-smoggy city on a rise. They do not, except on occasions like the Liberty anniversary that will soon be upon us, tend to sing hosannas. Actually, they are wont to grumble now and then.

But they do, by and large, when it counts, know that they are lucky. As conservatives, we need not ask any more of them. Or of ourselves.

—Midge Decter spoke at The Heritage Foundation on June 19, 1986. Hers was the first in a series of lectures on the question, "What Does It Mean to Be a Conservative?"

6 | Democracy and Freedom

O ne of our greatest difficulties in arriving at rational policies in our country, especially foreign policies, is the absence of a little old-fashioned straight and honest talk. Let me give you just one example–from the current hottest issue–of what I mean. Nowadays we find ourselves, quite suddenly at that, in what everybody is pleased to call a war on drugs. Why now, is an interesting question in itself: drugs, after all, have been killing off our kids for nearly a quarter of a century. One doubts that Nancy Reagan, commendable as her efforts have been, could have brought on this war by herself. But this is a question for another time. However it got going, this is one of the greatest tributes to public, shall we say, lack of candor that one has seen in an era that has produced many. While the great debate rages as to whether or not the military should be used to interdict the flow of drugs into this country; while pressure is put on the governments of the growers to let us, or help us, or to themselves undertake the destruction of the poppy and coca and cannabis crops; while authorities of various kinds fight with the so-called civil libertarians over whether people may or may not be tested–one critical, maybe *the* most critical thing is being overlooked. Among the people jumping up and down screaming that the government, especially Ronald Reagan, are not doing enough to prosecute this war are a lot of good middle-class American parents. And what they are really saying, underneath all the verbiage and outraged demands, and whether they know it or not, is: For God's sakes, the government had better *do* something about this threat to my children because I sure as hell am not going to. I can't or don't want to do anything about the demand problem. So you guys had better figure out how to cut off the supply.

Our brains are getting clogged with the chitchat of policy-makers intent on letting those who ought to be responsible for themselves off the hook.

This is not the only example of how our brains are getting clogged with the chitchat of policy-makers intent on letting those who ought to be responsible for themselves off the hook. There are hundreds of such examples. This is just one of the simplest. Which brings me to the subject of our discussion here today—another example of the absence of straight talk about responsibility. This one is a more complicated issue. Unlike drugs, democratization is a very complicated thing to talk about. It is complicated because the word democracy means both too little and too much. Usually what we mean by it, however, is simply majority rule. That is why we are always so intent upon the question of whether the countries we wish to democratize do or do not have elections. Now admittedly, for many of these countries an election is by itself already a big step. But for us, who live in the oldest genuine democracy on earth, elections are hardly even a beginning. They can produce a majority, but as our founding fathers understood when they were inventing our blessed Constitution, a majority can be a tyranny, and given human nature, usually does in fact become a tyranny unless it is reined in and checked. So right off the bat we have a problem with language that is serious and makes practical confusion. What we should be talking about is not democracy at all but freedom. They are not the same. Freedom can be incremental, it can be acquired gradually, in bits and pieces. As Jeane Kirkpatrick so brilliantly pointed out a long time ago, people have been known to enjoy more freedoms of a certain kind in some monarchies and even some dictatorships than they have in some so-called "democracies." Freedom is what it is people want for themselves. Moreover, freedom has a special compatibility with peaceableness, (it can also, alas, be diminished peacefully if people get too careless with it). In any case, people who go for democracy will not always get freedom. But free men will in the long run, if they are free enough and patient enough, create some form of decent democratic government for themselves. Real democracy, as distinct from the capacity to hold honest elections, takes a long time and requires genuine social stability. Let us not forget that our own democracy emerged from centuries of slowly grinding effort in a country called England. The American settlers who declared their independence had after all begun by demanding, as they themselves put it, the rights of free Englishmen.

> A majority can be a tyranny, and given human nature, usually does in fact become a tyranny unless it is reined in and checked.

So freedom, not democracy, is what the United States should be setting out to offer people. There is only one sure way we know of for a country to become a stable and prosperous democracy in just a few years. It is, however, a somewhat costly way, and not everyone can afford to try it–and anyway, by now, one can't even be sure it would work any more. That is the way the Japanese and the Germans did it. First, destroy yourself and get yourself occupied for a few years by the American army. The Israelis have a joke. One Israeli says to another: There is only one way for us to become rich and powerful, and that is, declare war on the United States and lose. Ah, says the other one, but suppose we don't lose? On second thought, this is no longer such of a joke.

> Seek out and identify our friends, the real living, breathing, flesh-and-blood friends of the United States, and embrace them in every way possible.

Since we can't wait for them to declare war on us so we can occupy them and create a government for them; and since it's not likely, at least in the near future, that we will even be doing what we did for the Dominican Republic and Granada, what can we do for those we wish to help and/or ally ourselves with in the so-called Third World? I am leaving Nicaragua out of the discussion here. That is by now a whole different question, and anyway you would not wish to see me weep so early in the morning in such a beautiful place as this.

It seems to me there are two things we can do. Both of them we are in fact already doing, but we are doing them feebly and inadequately. One is what Marc Plattner is involved in in the work of the National Endowment for Democracy, but this should be transformed from one of the President's little backwoods charities into a real and serious policy of the United States government. And that is: to seek out and identify our friends, the real living, breathing, flesh-and-blood friends of the United States, and embrace them in every way possible. Give them money, give them help, give them arms if they wish to and are able to use them, give them friendship. Above all, confirm for them the idea that it is a source of strength, not just a miserable losing proposition, to be supported by, and a supporter of, Uncle Sam. Contrary to the filthy propaganda purveyed every day in *The New York Times* and *The Washington Post*, America's real friends in the world—those businessmen, lawyers, and, yes, political prisoners, professors, journalists, who really understand and admire the American system and American society—in other words, those who are our friends out of conviction—are fine and worthy people. They need us. And we also need them. If our hopes for the world are ever to be realized, it will be because of them. This is true everywhere, not just in Central America. Too often, people are punished, or snubbed, or just neglected by American officialdom for being pro-American. It isn't just a matter of money, either, though if people are attempting to act as an opposition in a totalitarian country, they certainly need money from somewhere. But just as important, maybe more important—we have got to stop taking the heart out of them for the sin of being on our side.

The thing we first and foremost have to do for others at this juncture of human history is look after our own security.

That's the first thing. The second thing we need to do for freedom and democracy in Latin America—for the future of freedom and democracy throughout the world, including, I may say, Western Europe—the thing we first and foremost have to do for others at this juncture of human history is look after our own security. We're not very good at this these days; we've never been all that good at it, for a number of reasons. We didn't ask to be the leader of the free world; it was a job that history, you might say, stuck us with, and we are fundamentally an easy-going people who get no pleasure from, and are by now sick and tired of, living with our dukes up. Being a society fundamentally based on business, and thus profoundly under the influence of the ideas of practicality and good sense, we have an inadequate appreciation of the role of the irrational in human affairs. We think problems can be solved, and differences negotiated. We came through a period, after all not so very long ago, when between them the Nazis and Communists slaughtered around thirty million people–that is, not counting the ordinary casualties of war–and yet we do not yet, not really, believe that there is such a thing as evil. Ronald Reagan famously called the Soviets an evil empire. He took his lumps for it, too. But does Ronald Reagan really strike you as a man who has stared into the face of evil? He's too sunny, he's too amiable by nature, and he's too American. I do not mean to give one of those tiresome lectures on American naivety. And after all, our lack of acquaintance with evil derives from the fact that we live in a political system which has deprived us of the experience. But it does time after time leave us with a longing to chuck the whole business of world power and deceive ourselves into believing that we are not in danger. For forty years now we have been living with a rhythm of assuming our responsibilities for a few years and evading them for a few years, back and forth, and meanwhile we have talked, talked, talked, in an avalanche, a typhoon of high-flown words in the Congress, in the press, from the White House, until we are by now practically incapable of facing up to simple truths about ourselves and the world.

At this moment, when we have let so many people down in Central America, and given so much aid and comfort to our enemies, it seems to me worthwhile to say just a couple of plain and homely things about the U.S., democracy, and the Third World. We do not in truth know how to turn people into democrats. We know that a free-market economy is absolute necessary for this to happen, but it may not be sufficient, as elections are not by themselves sufficient. There are things that people have to do for themselves. Creating a lasting decent polity is one of them. On the other hand, we do if we let ourselves know a lot about freedom, about where it resides and about just how brave you have to be to sustain it. Soviet dissidents like Vladimir Bukovsky and Anatoly Sharansky and others have taught us that you can even, in your soul, be a free man in prison, far freer than your jailor.

In that sense, there are free men everywhere, probably in every country in the world. And if they are free, they look to us. They look to us for help of various kinds, as I said. We must give it to them to the extent we are humanly able. They look to us in another way as well, and here is where history itself is looking to us. They need us to be strong to be safe, they need us to be confident in the value of our own institutions. For in *our* strength and safety lies their reassurance that if they are brave enough one day to go through the anxieties of freedom, it will have been worthwhile. That is why they can hold elections every morning noon and night in El Salvador, or Guatemala, or Honduras, or Costa Rica, or you name it. If the United States is not strong and defended, and full of thanks for its own political blessings, the truly freedom-

> If the United States is not strong and defended, and full of thanks for its own political blessings, the truly freedom-loving men in those countries will not come to power, or if they do, will not stay there for long.

loving men in those countries will not come to power, or if they do, will not stay there for long.

Let me sum up the whole thing I am trying to say in one blunt sentence. The hope for freedom, and ultimately democracy, anywhere in the world, but especially Latin America, lies with a United States prepared to be the rich and powerful nation history appointed her to be. It's a terrible responsibility, and not much fun. It's a lot easier to make speeches at the U.N. and turn some money over to the World Bank. But there are worse fates for a country, as there are for an individual, than being called upon to be brave and good and strong and steady, to fight if need be, and to be grateful for blessings received.

—Midge Decter spoke at The Heritage Foundation's Board of Trustees meeting that took place June 16-18, 1988, on Peter Island, British Virgin Islands.

7 | Shaping a Foreign Policy Agenda for the 1990s

I want to talk about certain groups who are participating in this great new debate about foreign policy. To begin with, there are those whom I would call without the least bit of disrespect intended, but for the sake of brevity, the Endowment for Democracy Party.

These are the people who say we must consolidate our ideological and political winnings and push forward in a campaign to bring the blessings of democracy and the free market. (Have you ever noticed how funny it is that even to this day people are a little bit inhibited about using the word "capitalism"? So now we talk about the free market.) We must continue the effort to bring democracy to those ever-growing masses of people who are clamoring for it.

On the other side there are the isolationists, whose classic formulation from as far back as the country's founding has been, let us perfect ourselves and let our impact on the world, if any, be that of a model for envy and emulation.

And there are radical libertarians who are prepared to say that the rights of government should be so circumscribed as to make impossible any commitment beyond the literal defense of the country's own territory.

Somewhere along this spectrum, representing what I suspect is the largest constituency at this moment, are the party of the "Fed Up." Call them for short, the Pat Buchanan Party. Their view is one that no matter how much you disagree with it, it cannot fail to touch the nervous system and pluck the heartstrings. For more than 40 years, runs this argument, we pursued a policy which enabled our allies—not to speak of our World War II enemies—to get on their feet and then prosper mightily. And all the while as they depended on us to defend them, they hamstrung us, undermined our policies, in some cases—like Nicaragua—supported our enemies outright, and above all, subjected us to a continuing moral attack.

And now, more than a quarter of a million of our boys and girls are being forced to suffer the heat and tedium of Saudi Arabia, forbidden, as it were, to show their faces or fly their flag, in order to protect the supply of oil and the economies of these allies. Meanwhile, with the always honorable exception of Margaret Thatcher—and let us now hope of Prime Minister Major—they wring their hands in uncertainty as to how far they feel we should go in dealing with Saddam Hussein. Who can read the newspapers, at least some part of each week, without finding some reason or some occasion to say "the hell with the whole lot of them"? Emotion however, is not a policy nor does it even give guidance to it.

The fear of nuclear weapons is no doubt a perfectly legitimate emotion. One of the prominent policy suggestions it gave rise to, however, that the world would be a safer place if the United States had no nuclear weapons, does not even qualify as legitimate nonsense.

It will be objected that I have so far left out of this list the position, everybody's favorite in this town, of the hard-headed, national interest school—those who say that all foreign policy decisions are properly made only on the basis of a realistic calculation of the country's interests. The people who assume this position naturally believe themselves, and are able to behave as if they are, wiser, more worldly, more sophisticated than those who over the years earned for themselves the designation of anti-communist ideologues, like Senator Malcolm Wallop and like a few other people in this room.

The fear of nuclear weapons is no doubt a perfectly legitimate emotion. One of the prominent policy suggestions it gave rise to, however, that the world would be a safer place if the United States had no nuclear weapons, does not even qualify as legitimate nonsense.

There is a problem with the position of hard headedness however, and that is quite simply that it is entirely circular. For how can you hard headedly say what is the national interest at any given moment—especially should it be a moment of crisis—without some prior notion of what your belief is about and what your ambitions for the country are? And in addition, how you read the real and moral nature of the world?

For someone like me—who takes none of the positions I have just described, though I feel great emotional sympathy for all of them at different times—it seems that the first thing that has to be said on the subject of America's role in the world is that when you are the richest and most powerful nation on earth, and despite the best efforts of many of our social philosophers, educators and policy bureaucrats, we are still, and are likely to remain, the richest and most powerful nation on earth, it is pure fantasy to imagine that there is such an option for you as withdrawal from the affairs of other countries. There is no such thing as "non-intervention." If you decide to sit out some crisis, that is as much a form of intervention as sending troops. And in some cases, that can in the long run be even more dangerous. If the 20th Century has not taught the United States that lesson over and over in at least five different ways, then we are as a nation doomed forever to be casting around like a blind creature.

> When you are the richest and most powerful nation on earth, ...it is pure fantasy to imagine that there is such an option for you as withdrawal from the affairs of other countries.... If you decide to sit out some crisis, that is as much a form of intervention as sending troops.

The question, therefore, is not should we or shouldn't we intervene—but how. Now obviously there have been and will continue to be many crises in the world where it makes no sense for us to mix in. We might at any given moment differ about which these are or should be and why. Among serious people, that is what is called trying to arrive at a wise application of a policy. Should we try to help settle civil wars in Rwanda and Liberia? The prudent answer, at least for now, would seem to be no. And there are some conflicts—and I would say the Israeli–Palestinian conflict is one of those—for which there is simply nothing to be done by anyone but sit tight and wait for history to erode what are some of the key heated-up issues.

There are few assertions more specious, however, than the declaration that because we cannot or should not intervene in this place or that place at any given time, the obvious conclusion is that we must not intervene at all. Indeed, this kind of argument is not only specious, it's rather cheaply specious. Given the consequentiality of American conduct in the world–whether we will it or not– how should we understand that role now that 40-plus years of the organizing principle for American foreign policy is coming apart? Quite simply, history (or, if you will, fate) has ordained that we must play a key role in keeping international law and order; we must because there is no one else to do it.

I don't, in this auditorium of all places, have to say that the United Nations as an instrumentality for maintaining international comity has from almost the very first moment of its existence if not before that, been a farce. History may decide that the very worst policy of George Bush is, in fact, that he gave a new shot of energy to the United Nations.

And no more than on the streets of Washington or New York City can criminal conduct in the international arena be controlled without the belief that the authorities have power and are prepared to wield it. It is always to be hoped that the power and the readiness to use it will by themselves act as a deterrent. Often they do; we tend to forget that. Sometimes, on the other hand, they don't. Then what?

We can choose to ignore criminal acts. Again, if it is necessary to spell out the point in answer to those who say we cannot be the world's policeman, let me say that the criminal acts of which I speak are those that threaten the peace and security of whole neighborhoods in the world and ultimately, if not immediately, our own neighborhood. These crimes against the international order: we can ignore them, we can tell lies about them, we can deny to ourselves that they are taking place. Actually, we along with our Western allies at different times, have done all of these things—ignore, deny, or just plain lie.

We and our allies have done these things in particular because, as the late C.P. Snow once put it: "There is that in democratic peoples which hates the bearing of arms. It is a virtue and a dangerous weakness." And whenever we have denied or deceived ourselves, we have paid dearly. "Hitler had a legitimate right to a bit of *Lebensraum*," said our forebears in the 1930s. "Let him have the Rhineland, and later, the Sudetenland, and he will be satisfied."

There are many examples of this kind of highly costly sloth and self deception. To be sure, none so bloody or scarifying in outline as the British and French failure to deter a still weak Hitler in the 1930s. As for our presence in the Persian Gulf, if I felt I knew with any degree of certainty just what the Bush Administration has in mind there—and I don't think Mr. Bush himself knows any more by now—it would be easier to discuss this in such a context. But one thing is certain; we are there because a crime has been committed, a crime of the kind I described. Not only the invasion and rape of a small oil-rich kingdom on the Persian Gulf, but the threat of disruption to a whole already badly battered system of nations.

In a region vitally important both to the peace and the economic welfare of the world, it is constantly being said

by the isolationists, the libertarians, and the fed up that
we, the United States of America, have no serious interest
there, that if our allies, for instance, need oil, let them see
to their own problem, and so on and so on.

All very appealing and very tempting things to believe.
But oil is an issue for the entire world economy, and that
includes us—and that means women and children all over
the world, in poor countries as well as rich ones. Never,
never again should we let anybody
make the remark that our troops are
in Saudi Arabia to make the world
safe for gas guzzlers.

There is nothing more cynical that
anyone can say than that.

And there is another problem here.
The invasion of Kuwait was an act for
which we as Americans bear some
indeterminate but not small amount
of responsibility. Did not the American ambassador, certainly speaking
for the United States Department of
State (for ambassadors, after all, do not say such things on
their own), tell Saddam Hussein that the United States
would take no interest in the matter of an Iraqi invasion of
Kuwait? This assurance of our nonintervention was a
highly consequential factor. How could it be otherwise?
There is indeed no more poignant evidence that for the
U.S. nonintervention is a mirage than the role we played
in inciting the invasion of Kuwait.

So we have no choice but to play for now the central role in channeling the tides of world order. What we do have a choice about, however, is whether to play this role on purpose or inadvertently.

So we have no choice but to play for now the central role in channeling the tides of world order. What we do have a choice about, however, is whether to play this role on purpose or inadvertently. Iraq is the perfect example of playing it inadvertently, and we may not yet get out of it without a serious loss of life. I freely admit that without the organizing principle of anti-communism and the so-called *realpolitique* notwithstanding, it was anti-communism that held our policy together—and that brought its most notable successes, I might point out.

Without this principle, it will not be so easy to formulate an encompassing doctrine. Nevertheless, I for one am prepared to say that such a doctrine when it arrives, will bear a powerful resemblance to something called "Pax Americana." I know that term is one that is usually uttered only with a sneer; let me remind you, so was the term "free world" always spoken with a sneer.

This role will require us to be powerfully armed, a requirement about which we are already going to have a bitter political battle, but that will, if we are going to live in an even minimally peaceful world, may be more urgent than ever now.

Part of being powerfully armed is of course, being powerfully defended, a requirement receding further and further from us every day. I was recently at a meeting where people were speaking and cheering about SDI, and my heart was breaking because Strategic Defense Initiative was sailing off into the sunset before our very eyes.

We cannot have the wisdom to know at every moment what to do, and we will make mistakes of course—but these mistakes will not be fatal, as long as we are prepared to acknowledge the real weight of our responsibility. And one thing more. Let us carry the burden of that responsibility with confidence, and this not only refers to Congress, this refers to all of us. All of us who attempt to influence public opinion.

Pax Americana will not be some dark imperialist conspiracy; the further we carry the force of the American political culture and spread the influence of American political institutions, a better place the world will be.

Russians know that, Ukrainians know that, Poles know that. Why don't we know it? Once again, the main job of convincing people about the legitimacy of American aims will be here at home—and that job is up to us.

—Midge Decter spoke at
The Heritage Foundation on December 3, 1990.

8 | What We Are to Do

I'm afraid I have to ask you to forgive me in advance for the things I am going to talk about today and the way I am going to talk about them. A couple of months ago Gary Bauer and I were having a conversation about the terrible state of the ethos of the so-called advanced and enlightened community in the United States. Gary, as many of you probably know, served as an advisor on domestic policy in the Reagan White House and has now become a crusader within the Family Research Council. And I, it will not surprise you to learn, am a typical and well-practiced old-fashioned grandmother. There we were, Gary the crusader and I the grandmother, commiserating with one another about the difficulty of forcing people to see just how truly terrible things are, and together we came to the conclusion that we were hamstrung by the requirements of good manners and refinement, and that the only way to sound certain alarms properly was by talking in a way that many people we respect and care for are apt to find offensive. You can't fully discuss the famous issue of the photographs of Robert Mapplethorpe, for example, if you cannot uneuphemistically describe for people the images of a man urinating into another man's mouth or a man with the handle end of a bull whip stuck into his anus. Further, you cannot truly discuss the cultural weight of these photographs if you are for some reason inhibited about saying, not merely that they are disgusting, outrageous, debased, and decadent, but that they constitute, preeminently and *par excellence*, the imagery of homosexuality. (Even the redoubtable and admirable Jesse Helms was not quite up to making an emphatic point of *that*.)

So here we are, encamped in this virtual daydream of a tropical paradise, engaged in discussing what has, in all honesty, to be a lot of extremely nasty stuff. That's the trouble with talking about the state of our culture. It would have been much more amusing to talk about, say, the effects of nuclear war. Well, dedicating this talk in spirit to my friend Gary Bauer, who unlike me is young and pure of heart and brave enough to spend every day of his life wading through the muck, I'm afraid you are going to find me a bit brutal, and I apologize for it.

> The welfare system has created a powerful incentive for women not to marry or set up any permanent housekeeping with the fathers of their children and now way more than half the babies born to poor black young women are illegitimate.

My assignment is to talk about the government-created culture of dependency and its destructive impact on families. Well, that's not *too* bad; we all know what the government policy involved here is. It's the welfare system, particularly Aid to Families with Dependent Children, and we all know its impact on families among the poor people served by the welfare system. It has not been news for more than twenty years that the welfare system has created a powerful incentive for women not to marry or set up any permanent housekeeping with the fathers of their children and that now way more than half the babies born to poor black young women, especially if they are poor young women, are illegitimate. By now, they constitute a third, moving into a fourth, generation. And if these young women are motivated not to marry, they have no incentive to concern themselves with the question of chastity, so motherhood appears to be arriving in their lives earlier and earlier. This is not news, as I said; even the *New York Times* has seen fit to publish it. The question then arises, what are we to do about it? And here comes the parade of policies: make welfare recipients work; make them have abortions; give them plenty of free condoms, and instructions in how to use them beginning, let us say, in the fourth grade; establish more drug treatment centers; improve the quality of education; and so on. Some of these policies may be good ones, some are clearly monstrous. But what they all have in common is that they are large and general and thus soothingly distanced from the reality they are intended to alter. Spend just one hour hanging around an inner-city street corner, for instance, and you will see just how sad and feeble are the very words "job opportunity program." The young men you see on that corner don't want jobs-unless you call selling your girlfriend a job-and couldn't keep them for two hours if they did. Or ride on a New York City bus in midafternoon, after high school has let out, and eavesdrop on the conversations of those teen-age mothers, some of them already the mothers of two: they don't want abortions and they don't want contraceptives-and believe me, they know about both. What they want is the passivity, the will-lessness, that brought the babies upon them in the first place. Their life is decided *for* them, not *by* them. I don't think the welfare system by itself created that desire for passivity for them-it comes from something very deep-but the welfare system has encouraged them and indulged them in it and helped to harden it from a wish-and who among us has not wished some time not to have to be responsible for oneself?–for them the wish is hardened into a lifelong mode of existence.

A few of these young unwed mothers will, one way or another, or as a result of one program or another, escape. There is for these girls, as there is not for their unformed, undeveloped, basically emasculated boyfriends, the possibly saving fact that having babies around at least makes you get up out of bed in the morning. I would emphasize the word "possibly" because we can almost not imagine any more the widespread, commonplace, unspeakable neglect and brutality wreaked upon the children of these non-families. How many have been left alone for days to starve or asphyxiate themselves or be burned to death, how many merely brutalized, physically and emotionally? You see, even the expression "the culture of dependency" is a euphemism. We all know in our bones what that culture has become, and dependency is hardly an adequate word to summon the true horror meant by it.

Let me make good the threat contained in my initial apology and set before you the family story that is in its field the equivalent of a Mapplethorpe photo. This is the story of a 12-year old girl in Brooklyn, an orphan who has been living with her crack-addicted aunt and her aunt's now 16-year-old stepson. Three weeks or so ago this little girl gave birth to a baby boy, whom, with umbilical cord still attached, she put into a shopping bag and dropped down the garbage chute of her building. At the bottom of this chute was a compactor, which was just about to be turned on when the maintenance men heard the baby cry and searching through the garbage found him, alive and apparently unhurt. The baby was rushed to a hospital, and the mother was arrested. A day or two later, the 16-year-old boy in the household went up to the roof and was there caught in the act of attempting suicide. His family, he said by way of explanation, was against him. These bare facts were all the authorities made public—mercifully: how much more could one bear to know?

Now tell me the program, the policy, the public initiative or even the private one, that speaks adequately to this story. To be sure, it is an extreme case, but only in the sense that a Mapplethorpe photograph is an extreme case of homosexual aestheticism. Did the government have a hand in it? Surely. But then, so did we all.

Oh dear. Is this one of those "We are guilty" speeches? And is she just going to leave us this way, everything is beyond repair and there's nothing to be done? The answer to both these questions is no. We have all had a hand in this story in the sense that it is a story not about legislation nor about economics and not even entirely about policy per se but about culture: late 20th-century American, which is to say liberal, culture—which precedes and underlies the legislation and policy.

And there is much we can do—and even more we can stop doing (sometimes stopping something is more important than positive action, like giving up a bad habit)—there are things we can do and stop doing to help promote the process of healing. Notice I said *help*. When you have a cultural problem defined as dependency—I think it more accurately defined as irresponsibility—you have to recognize that it is a problem or condition which must be confronted and dealt with precisely by those who are afflicted with it.

So what are *we* to do?

A lot of the things we have to do we have to do with our hearts and minds first. The policies—if any in fact apply—will follow. And with our hearts and minds we have to recognize that the culture which is corrupting and crippling the children of the ghetto is the same culture as the one in which we all live. We may have our immunities to that culture, as the children of the ghetto do not, but we live in it nevertheless and too often—much, much too often—we have made our peace with it. The chief message of that culture, the message that is destroying America's poor, and is not doing such wonderful things for our own children and grandchildren either, is the liberal message that life is not supposed to be hard and that if it is, it's somebody's fault: the government, the racists, the sexists, the rich, the poor, the landlords, you name it. Our sins are someone else's, our mistakes are someone else's, and our misfortunes only happened because someone failed preemptively to avert them. We could discuss where this idea, or these ideas, came from, but that would take us too far afield. The point is, they are the bedrock of the liberal civilization we are living in, and calling ourselves conservatives does not protect us from it.

We have been reduced—to concentrate specifically on the corner of this problem that I have been assigned to talk about today–we have been reduced to saying we are for the family. *For* the family?!? You mean those squalling kids who take forever to grow up and then just as soon as they do fly the coop completely? You mean Aunt Gertie who is not on speaking terms with Uncle Willie because he inherited the silverware? To say you are for the family–you might as well say you are for the clouds or the rocks or the trees. I submit that we find ourselves in the ridiculous position of defending the family, as they say, because it took us all so very long to recognize how dangerous were the assaults on it over the years, and

No-fault divorce means no-promise marriage.

because when we did recognize them, we mainly sat back wringing our hands. How different was it really for example, for the liberal ideologues to bring about the institution of no-fault divorce? No-fault divorce means no-promise marriage. What about the equal-rights amendment, which went through Washington like a knife through butter and but for Phyllis Schlafly–and I mean that literally–but for Phyllis Schlafly, would have been ratified in short order while many too many of us were saying, well, what's wrong with equal pay for equal work? Who was prepared to make a serious and important argument for keeping young women out of the service academies–with the result we saw only yesterday: mothers kissing their two- and three-month-old babies goodbye and going off to the Gulf War: in the name of, as the result of, something that had once been declared–*uncontested*–to be a noble principle. And where but Georgetown University was there anything approaching a really serious battle over full campus recognition of a gay student organization, by which, let us face it, what we are talking about is official university funding for student sodomy. It would be interesting to know just how many colleges and universities suffered a decline in funding over the recognition of gay organizations on campus, either from state legislatures or from private donors. I would suspect the answer is, not one. (P.S. Georgetown I need hardly say, basically gave in in the end.) The meaning of those gay groups being officially recognized is that we are a society no longer willing even to *define* what is a family, let alone honor it, let even more alone, to take it for granted.

That is not the government, my friends, that is us, us Americans, a people in a state of deep contradiction. We are the most God-fearing, church-going nation in the world, who have yet been unable to muster the arguments, and the strength of will to go with them, to resist the imposition on our society of an unholy, I would call it Satanic decadence. *That* is what is meant by the term "cultural crisis."

Let us return to our 12-year-old. We cannot forget her or she will kill us all. It is true that we are limited in what we can do for her, but what is left within those limits is essential. She is being destroyed–in her particular, individual case, of course, she has already been detroyed–by an idea: the idea is that she is a victim and nothing but a victim and if someone doesn't do for her–someone: the system, the social workers, the teachers, the abortionists, *someone*–nothing can be expected of her and she need not expect anything of herself. This is a very liberal idea, a very sinful idea, and it was permitted to eat into the moral sinew of our society for years and years before the first serious, hopeful counteraction against it gathered any strength. We must fight that idea in all its manifestations as loudly and unapologetically as we can.

But in order to fight it on her behalf we have to fight it on our own. The main thing we can do for that girl's little friends who have not yet murdered and gone to jail–and by we, I mean those of us who know that families do not come in nineteen delicious flavors but are in all their limitations, indeed precisely *because* of all their limitations, the necessary humanizing ground on which to live–the most important thing we can do for *every*one of *every* class and circumstance being crippled by liberal culture and confirmed in their handicap by the policies that go with it is stand up for ourselves, for what we are and what we know and how we live. The methods employed to silence us are legion, including name-calling, smearing, distortion, defamation, and on campuses nowadays, straight and open censorship.

We know, as the liberals do not, that we are all morally equal in the sight of God, and will all ultimately answer to the same judgement.

So we have *got* to establish some line of communication, through, or around, the liberal culture, between us and those girls having babies and those boys fleeing manhood. For we, and not the government and not the social workers, are their hope: not for what we can do for them but for what we are, people willing to hold them to a stern standard and who believe, as the liberals do not, that if we and they are stern enough, they will one day be able to lead decent lives. People who know, as the liberals do not, that we are all morally equal in the sight of God, and will all ultimately answer to the *same* judgement.

It's terrible to have to make a movement to say what ought not even to need saying. Without idealizing them in any way, it's fair to say our parents didn't need to say these things. And maybe if we are brave enough and steady enough and insistent enough, our grandchildren won't need to say them either. Meanwhile we have a very hard and dirty and enlivening and invigorating job to do.

—Midge Decter spoke at The Heritage Foundation's
Board of Trustees meeting that took place April 17-19, 1991,
on Peter Island, British Virgin Islands.

9 | Why American Families Are So Unhinged

When I was invited to come here to speak to you on the subject of women and/or family values, I must confess to you that my response was, "I hate to talk about women, and family values is a crock." First of all, I abominate the word values. (As in, my values are what I happen to prefer and they are better than your values, which are what you happen to prefer. Or even believe in.) I should have thought that the late Allan Bloom had put that word to rest forever in any field outside of mathematics and chemistry. Furthermore, in my opinion there is no such subject as women; we are all in this together, men, women, and children. And I'm not too crazy about the word family either. I always want to know what people mean by that. When the conversation gets around to family, I want to ask, "What do you mean by family? Sisters and brothers not on speaking terms because of a quarrel over property? People who presume to invade your privacy merely because they have known you since you were a small and helpless child? People who will never forget that you once bit your nails or wet your bed?"

Well, of course, I don't really feel as flippant as that sounds. It is in fact not a matter of flippancy at all but rather of astonishment that we should have gotten ourselves into the kind of mess where we should be speaking of family as if its existence were something to have opinions and theories about. Families, as I believe I have said many times before in these precincts, just ARE, the way nature just is. Sometimes they are good news and sometimes, let us not forget, they are bad news, but they are not up for debate. Why, then, are we debating about the family as if its existence were somehow open to our determination? How did we ever come to this? That's the question I really want to talk to you about.

> F amilies, as I believe I have said many times before in these precincts, just ARE, the way nature just is.

Now, by way of answer I begin with what I suspect is the real beginning, namely, the proposition that in discussions of American life there is no single word used as often and as automatically as the word "change." (And given the newly installed Clinton administration, we probably ain't seen nothin' yet.) We Americans seem to have a special penchant for thinking about ourselves, for measuring ourselves, for keeping a running account of our condition, for, as you might say, taking the national temperature at regular intervals. And in all this measuring and temperature-taking, the one idea that remains constant is the idea of change.

Merely from reading the daily papers over the past forty years, you would have the impression that we have been through more fundamental revolutions—revolution, of course, being another term in popular use among us—than the world had seen in the preceding thirty centuries. We are, in short, a people besotted with our courtship of the new.

Many of you in this room may be too young to remember a man named Marshall McLuhan. He was a very brilliant and original man, who like many brilliant and original men, was afflicted with the sinful temptation to be profound. He looked at us all watching television (television was in those days still new enough to theorize about) and claimed to see in it not a marked change in public habits of recreation—which television certainly was—but nothing less than a radical change in the very nature of human perception. Henceforth we would not only be spending, or if you will, wasting, a good deal of time in the company of this new technology, we would be nothing less than a new species of people. Need I tell you that before he vanished into social theory heaven, he was touted as the new thinker of our age?

McLuhan is perhaps an extreme example—though he is by no means the only one nor, perhaps, even the most extreme. And certainly in many seemingly milder forms we are constantly being invited—and just as constantly accepting each new invitation—to see ourselves as travelers embarked on some uncharted sea, all alone, without a compass. Just in the last thirty years, we have had the sexual revolution, the youth revolution, the pseudo-existentialists' revolution of consciousness, the revolution from producerism into consumerism, the death of nationalism, the transmogrification of the planet into spaceship earth, and, of course, most relevant to our discussion today, the death-of-the-family, or, even more recently, anything-is-a-family, revolution.

And with each of these revolutions there has come, inevitably, the birth of a new generation. American society has become a veritable miracle of procreation. It used by common calculation take thirty years to produce a new generation; we produce at least one every five years. How we do this with so low a birthrate might once have been the subject for deep scientific speculation. But the answer is really quite simple. We produce these rapidly accelerating generations not by conception and birth but by journalism. Generations are found by the press and media, you might say, full grown, under the mulberry bushes of pop social theory.

> We produce these rapidly accelerating generations not by conception and birth but by journalism.

And in the end, paradoxically, the one thing that truly makes us different from our forebears is the effect on us of this willingness, nay eagerness, to accept the idea that we are changed.

And what is the effect on us that I am referring to? In plain language, it is driving us nuts.

Let me give you just a few of the more colorful examples of what I mean. In most places in this country, the automobile has become the exclusive means of getting from one place to another. People jump into their cars to go to the nearest corner. If one's battery goes dead or, say, one's carburetor needs adjustment, full-scale emergency measures must be taken. In Beverly Hills, California, I am told, if someone is seen walking in a residential neighborhood, he is immediately suspected by the police. Yet every morning and every evening, and sometimes in the middle of the night, hundreds of thousands, maybe millions, of people don special costumes and shoes and at serious risk to ankles, shins, and spines run miles and miles to nowhere in particular and back again.

These same people, or others indistinguishable from them, have recently discovered that some foods have more beneficial nutrient properties than others. They have taken to considering and weighing every single thing they put into their mouths. There are never fewer than two diet books on *The New York Times* best seller list (not all of them, by the way, about how to get thin or be beautiful; some tell you how to eat so you can enjoy eternal life, and some tell you how to eat so you can succeed in business). We are, moreover, routinely issued dire warnings about what will kill you: the wrong food, the wrong air, the poisoned earth, the failure of the federal government to find the cure for this, that, and the other disease—which we hear each night over the airwaves is killing one out of every ten, or seventy, or eight hundred Americans each minute of each year. You would think the government is killing us all with its neglect. And yet everywhere we look there are old people, older than we have ever known, trying to find something to do with themselves, preferably in warm climates. Still, we walk around trembling over our imminent deaths.

Here's another example. As we all know, a critical aspect of our lives nowadays is "relationship." Some people call it "communication." People go to great lengths and vast expenditures of money to learn how to relate to one another. They even study it in college. They touch, they feel, they hug, they look into one another's eyes, on cue, as instructed to do. Yet the very same people, in ever increasing numbers, are to be seen—at work, at play, and simply walking down the street—with their ears plugged up and connected to a little box in their pockets, eyes rolling heavenward, fingers snapping. People with Walkmans—and their number is by now legion—are people marching each to his own separate and solitary drummer. You cannot even reach them to say, "Excuse me, but you are standing on my foot."

A group of young, well-heeled American women—the best educated, healthiest, freest, and most benignly brought up women in the history of the world—startled everyone by announcing in no uncertain terms that they were the victims of intolerable oppression.

Now, moving from the sillier to the more advanced forms of derangement, a number of years ago, a group of young, well-heeled American women—the best educated, healthiest, freest, and most benignly brought up women in the history of the world—startled everyone by announcing in no uncertain terms that they were the victims of intolerable oppression. Chief among their oppressors, they told us, were their men: their fathers, brothers, professors, lovers, husbands. It seems that these men were treating them in a manner they dubbed "macho." Macho to them meant an excess of masculine ego and brutality. Macho men, the complaint ran, were keeping women on a pedestal, treating them on the one hand like little China dolls, and on the other hand, keeping them slaves and slapping them around. On one level, the complaint was that men were claiming for themselves the exclusive right to be powerful, to be breadwinners and competitors. On another level, it was that men refused to be tender and were afraid to cry. The response of the men to this indictment—and following them, the response of all the institutions of the culture—was immediate and unmistakable:

first nervous resignation, expressed mainly in a kind of embarrassed giggle, then coerced assent, and finally full capitulation. With an almost astonishing alacrity, the men set out to mend their ways. They knocked down the pedestals; they began to shrink from the competition; and they commenced as well to duck out on the breadwinning. And as an earnest of their good intentions, they also began to cry. If whining and apologizing count for crying, they cried a lot.

Now, it may or may not amaze you to learn, the chief indictment of young, educated middle-class women against men is that they are wimps. One now hears women demanding in those wonderful proving-grounds of human delicacy, the television talk-shows and the style-section features, where are the *men*? And think of it: all this wonderful revolutionary progress was accomplished in less than twenty years!

One important effect of this remarkably speedy accomplishment has been the effect on what is arguably the most widely publicized of all our recent revolutions, namely, the sexual revolution. Unlike many of the others, the sexual revolution appears to be a permanent, and permanently evolving, one. Originally, the sexual revolution meant that women were now free to have as much premarital—and in some quarters also extramarital—sexual experience as men. It meant the lifting of the terrible old double standard. It also meant that women were to have the same sexual experience as men. They could pursue as well as be pursued, and for every male climax, there had to be at least one female one. In aid of this revolution, responsibility for contraception was shifted from men to women; manuals of sexual performance proliferated; college dormitories became coeducational; the terms of parental guidance on these matters, if there were any at all, were radically altered; and, as was to be expected, the popular culture fell completely into line. But no sooner had young women, in obedience to these revolutionary aims, begun to sleep around than they declared a counter-revolution. It was called Women's Lib. Liberation for women now meant not liberation to have sex but liberation *from* sex. The original revolution, they said, so far from liberating them, had merely made them slaves to men's filthy lusts. To make matters even more confusing, the move from revolution to counterrevolution took place so rapidly that most young girls were actually taking part in both at the same time. Simultaneously they were jumping in and out of beds and being as hostile as possible about it. The result, not uncommon to revolutions I suppose, has been open and bloody warfare between young men and young women. No wonder they are marrying late and divorcing often.

So I guess you could say at the very least that things are not exactly well with us. Consider the following two curiosities: I do not remember the precise statistics, but they are impressive: rarely does one reach college nowadays— and even more rarely does one leave college nowadays— without having some, and possibly a considerable amount of, sexual experience. Yet while this very development was taking place, the country was at the same time being virtually smothered in pornography. If, as most people believe, pornography lives on, and feeds on, and is an expression of, sexual repression, how do we put together these two developments? American children were freed to become sexually active in order that they should not have to suffer the diseases of repression that once allegedly afflicted their elders and enriched a whole generation of psychoanalysts. Yet a moment's glance at any newsstand, or at the shelves of any videotape rental shop, or at late-night cable television, would suggest that at least this disease of a persistently repressed sexuality is running ever more rampant.

Or take the even more consequential problem of birth control and abortion. At a time when contraception has become both extremely effective and simple and easily available, in a certain number of American cities abortions are each year outnumbering live births. Say what you will about abortion—that it is murder or that it is no more than every woman's natural right—even the most passionate pro-choice advocate will not maintain that abortion is the preferred method of birth control. Yet again these two developments—an ever more perfected contraception and ever more widespread abortion—have gone hand in hand. Each year the experts produce whole libraries devoted to a dissection of the way we live now. But there has not been a single effort to explain to us how it is that sexual freedom and easy contraception should come attended with so much pornography and so many abortions.

> These two developments—an ever more perfected contraception and ever more widespread abortion—have gone hand in hand.

I have cited these examples, perhaps from the trivial to the deeply important—and they are by no means all the examples that could be cited—to underscore my assertion that there is something haywire with us.

The truth is, we Americans do live in very different circumstances from those of most of mankind throughout history and even today throughout the rest of the world. But we are as human beings constituted no differently. Women, to take one of my own earlier examples, do not really wish to jump in and out of a wide variety of beds and do not thrive when they do so. Women do not thrive, either, when they live at war with men. Nor do men thrive when they are forced to live at war with women.

The circumstances under which we live are not only different, they are unbelievably benign. We live longer. We are healthier. Most of us do not have to stand by helplessly as our children are being ravaged by disease and other disasters of nature. We are mobile. The whole world in all its variety and fascination is open to us.

Still, we are troubled and we are right to be so. It is not the fact of change that troubles us so but our belief in change. For in our daily affairs we have come to conduct ourselves as if we were quite free to make up our own rules and our own lives. Each of us is a kind of walking Ford Foundation research grant to study an as yet uncompleted social experiment.

That is how this issue called family got to be put on the table. A number of years ago, a White House conference on the family—a gathering of people respectable enough to be invited by their President to advise him—foundered on the conferees' inability to agree on what is a family: is it a mother and a father living together with their offspring, or two fathers or two mothers living with their offspring, or just any collectivity of people living under the same roof in a loving way—or perhaps, for that matter, in an unloving way? The question of definition, as we know, has since then been moved out of conference, so to speak, and into the courts. So judges of all people will now decide what and who constitute a family.

The only proper response to all this, it seems to me, is, *"Are they all crazy?"* Define a family? Haven't we all got enough trouble with the family we've got? Kids who are a pain in the neck? Parents who, no matter how old and accomplished you are, go on telling you to wipe your nose? Endless days and nights of worry—about money, about the future, about whether one is doing the right thing? No wonder, once you start talking about the "value of families" you go off the track. Families are not something good, like chocolate cake, families are absolutely necessary. They are necessary not to make you happy but to make you *human.* To be human beings worthy of the name, we live in a perpetual onrushing tide of generation, taking from those who went before and giving in return to those who come after. That's what family teaches. Without that, you could live in a crowd and you'd still be a solitary atom, facing a senseless death foreshadowed by a weightless life. Fancy trying to fit that into a political campaign! We know what the politicians mean by the term family values, especially what the Republicans mean. They mean among other things no condoms and no introduction to homosexuality and no teaching about anal sex in the schools. And had they talked straight, who knows? They might have electrified the country. But when politicians adopt an issue, you

> Families are not something good, like chocolate cake, families are absolutely necessary. They are necessary not to make you happy but to make you human.

can bet the farm that it will always come disguised as something abstract and toothless. I don't care what party you belong to or support, if you are trying to overcome any of the sorrows of our culture, you had better look elsewhere than to the politicians.

Each of us indeed had better begin by looking inside his own mind. For each of the heralds of change, each of the so-called revolutions that keep getting declared on our behalf carries the subliminal message that we late-twentieth-century Americans are unlimited and infinitely malleable. The result has been—certainly in the case of my generation it has—that we no longer assume the onerous burden of trying to teach our children what life truly requires of people. We pretend to ourselves to believe that in a technologically altered world no one way to conduct oneself is necessarily better or more useful than any other. We carry on about threats to our health and well-being when we are healthier and better off than anyone because we have in truth grown sick. And the etiology of this sickness is the denial that there are any limits on us. We keep defining things—sex, family, nature itself—in keeping with our constantly altering preferences, and the result is a kind of inescapable vertigo—call it a spiritual inner-ear infection.

In the 1960s our children confronted us—and here the "us" is the educated middle class in general and us, me myself and my friends, in terrible particular. Our children confronted us, their parents, their teachers, their spiritual leaders, their political leaders, and said, We don't want the life you offer us. It's too boring and hard. It's too dangerous. It's too...grown-up. We want, as my three-year-old grandson would put it, another different one. And what did we—all of us, parents, teachers, ministers and rabbis, politicians—what did we say in reply? "Suit yourselves." That's what we said.

To be sure, nowadays in universities the kids are not being told to suit themselves—at least not by their educators. Many of these teachers, as we know, were the young folk of the '60s I was talking about, and they seem to have determined that the freedom stops with them—that their students will have to make do, intellectually and socially, with what has turned out to suit *them*. But no matter how coerced to march in lockstep, students today are also the spiritual children of change—if for no other reason than that they too are being asked to choose a position on issues as bedrock as sex and family.

People, even the freest people on earth, cannot make their own rules and cannot make up their own lives. They cannot revolutionize themselves by fiat, merely by declaring to one another that they have done so. We need to live in communities, communities of families, if you will. We need to be affirmed and supported by others. We need to give ourselves to others. We need above all to accept the boundaries of our nature. Otherwise there is no telling just how batty—batty and unhappy—we and our children and our children's children will end up being.

—Midge Decter spoke at
The Heritage Foundation on April 8, 1993,
as part of the W.H. Brady Lecture Series
on Defining Conservatism.

10 | The State of Our Culture

My friends, you see before you this morning someone in a certain state of perplexity. I am what some people at least would call a good citizen: I do not speed, or park illegally, and I do not litter. While it is true that I have been known to display a certain indifference to the plight of spotted owls—not to mention foxes, raccoons, and especially minks—I am at least not mean to dogs and cats. I do not cheat on my taxes, and since I live in New York City, not to mention New York State, you should understand that that means a whole lot of not cheating. And I did not vote for Hillary Clinton. Yet here I am, talking to a group of people who are collectively my favorite people in this world, and the only subject they could think of for me to talk to you about is that very noisome and irksome problem that goes by the name of culture. Perhaps some day they will let me talk about something more pleasant, like economic recession or what to do about North Korea.

Of course, when I tell you that my topic is American "culture," I do not mean what ought to be meant by the term, that is, the way most people living in the United States think and feel and behave toward one another. That might be a whole lot of fun to think and talk about, for American culture in that sense is positively fascinating and various and full of wonderful bits of gold. But no. My assignment today is to talk about culture in the other, very far from amusing, sense: namely, the way a particular gang of very powerful and influential people have for a long time now been insisting that Americans should think and feel and behave toward one another. They are not so numerous, these powerful people, but they have succeeded in making so much noise that the rest of us can barely hear ourselves trying to think our own sensible thoughts. To the point, indeed, where describing this din has become rather like sending out dispatches from the midst of an artillery battle.

And that theater of operations called culture, through no intention on the part of most of us, is the place to which we have now been dragged, fighting—it is no exaggeration to say—for our very lives. That we had no wish to be here, however, does not, I am afraid, make us entirely blameless for our present predicament. For too long too many of us hoped, or pretended, that all those influential people—the press, the media, the universities, the bureaucrats, the intellectuals—were not really all that powerful, that they would somehow go away, or that we could get rid of them by outvoting them (as in fact we regularly enough do). In this, we were not unlike the United States itself at the end of World War II, when we brought the boys home and danced in the streets, and then had to mobilize all over again. But when it comes to culture in the sense I have been assigned to talk about today, hoping, and even voting, count for little; what matters—again as at the end of World War II—are the facts on the ground—or in the present case, the ideas in the air.

When did all this noise—and the bloody battles it presaged—start? It would be hard to answer this question in fewer than ten large tomes, but let me sketch just a few of the early warnings.

In the 1960s, the cadre of cultural spokesmen I described before began to announce that "our young people"—for which read *their* young people—were the most brilliant, the most gifted, and the most idealistic youths the world had ever seen. That they were busy trashing their universities, especially the libraries thereof; that they were singing hymns to drugs; that many of them were running off to communes or even simply nice vacation spots, such as San Francisco, Taos, or Aspen—where, incidentally, they were living on checks from home or, in the cases where such checks did not materialize, on welfare; that they were falsely claiming to be homosexual or crazy in order to avoid the draft; that they were timing their so-called peace demonstrations to coincide with their exam weeks, thereby making clear the true depth of their idealism; and finally and most horribly, that they were committing suicide in unprecedented numbers; all this made no difference to the major spokesmen of our culture. All the while these so-called "kids" were doing these things under our very noses, they were still being proclaimed the best and the brightest. Their standards, it was said, were simply too high to permit of their taking up their parents' dreary, suffocating lives of getting and spending. And as I said, many too many of us sat by and watched as our children and their friends were being trained in their schools and universities, in song and story, to serve as cannon fodder for all the devilish liberal pretensions of the age. You think that

Too many of us sat by and watched as our children and their friends were being trained in their schools and universities, in song and story, to serve as cannon fodder for all the devilish liberal pretensions of the age.

what we are teaching you is a bunch of irrelevant—to use their word for it—crap? said their educators. How wonderful of you to say so; we surrender. And the media, and the press, and many, tragically many, of their own parents followed suit—or pretended to.

At about the same time there came along a company of radical blacks, community organizers and politicians, who in the name of justice set about depriving their constituents of both the ambition and the courage necessary to achieving the lives that would have brought them into full partnership in American society. Blacks are oppressed, said their putative spokesmen, therefore dish them out some bogus equality in the form of unearned perks and jobs—to be administered, of course, by us. Do not educate the children, they said, merely pity them, make excuses for them, and above all, do not expect anything of them. Give them what we will all agree to call self-esteem by handing us political power and jobs. And need I say that these so-called "leaders" are still at it—perhaps more so than ever. After all, as the late Bayard Rustin once so memorably remarked, "Oppression pays." It is an understatement to say that the cultural arbiters of this society raised not a finger to oppose this crime against black children. Nor have they found the heart to do so until this very day, even as we witness the fruit of their ideas in such happy symptoms as drive-by shootings and an ever-growing cohort of fatherless (and often nowadays also motherless) babies.

As the late Bayard Rustin once so memorably remarked, "Oppression pays."

Then there were the women. Ah, the women. Using the pretext of the demand for equality, a group of the luckiest, healthiest, most prosperous, best educated, and most kindly treated young women in the history of the world declared open warfare on men, on motherhood, on nature itself (including, though some people are surprised to hear it, sex). Once again everyone sat by—especially men: fathers, husbands, boy friends, bosses—watching passively with barely a murmur of protest while a completely gratuitous and deep-seated misery set in. Now we have reached the point where the back sections of even the most respectable magazines are given over to pages and pages of personal ads placed by women seeking men and men seeking women. Once upon a time this kind of advertising was exclusively given over to invitations to various forms of illicit and kinky sex—and was carried in the kind of publications that arrived in the mail in brown paper wrappers: "Couple in Toronto," one of these ads might say, "seeking like-minded friends for parlor games; p.s., we play both ways, watchers invited." Or something to that effect, usually somewhat more graphic than my example. But who cared? Such people lived in a different world from ours and were happy to stay out of our way, and out of mind. The ads I am speaking of now are quite new and speak to a major, and growing, social disturbance. The advertisers are perfectly respectable people, and their claims and invitations evoke a spreading inability of men and women, young and not young, to get together, or having once got together, to negotiate the kind of settlement that would enable them to stay that way. The ads are written, to save space, in a kind of shorthand: "YSWF [which stands for young single white female] attractive and fun-loving, loves to dance, seeks man 30 to 40 for fun and romance, with a possible view to commitment." Or it might be "DWPF" [divorced white Protestant female] or SJF [single Jewish female] "mature, full-figured, opera-lover seeks the company of S or D mature, sympathetic male who likes to travel. Non-smoker required." I could go on and on with such examples, but you get the point. I urge you, in any case, if you have not already done so, to read a page or two of these ads, for your education. In a way, even more interesting are the ads from the men, many of whom announce them-selves to be lawyers, stockbrokers, accountants, doctors. Here is a char-acteristic specimen taken from a recent issue of *New York Magazine*: "Head for Surgery, Heart for Love—an outgoing, fun, 'old-fashioned good guy,' handsome, prominent MD, sophisticated, 39, fit, tall, mega-successful—seeks warm, pas-sionate, charming lady under 37, who finds meaning in building a relationship and family. Note/photo necessary." Seeking, seeking, seeking: fun, companionship, commit-ment, romance, sympathy—all the things that flirting and courtship were once the means for working out. But plain old flirting and courtship, in this age of bad temper and sexual harassment lawsuits, is no longer an available option. Where did they come from, all these educated, accomplished, respectable—and desperately lonely people? Read and weep: they are the casualties of a pointless and destructive, but too long unresisted, war between the sexes. They may not seem as urgent a social problem as, say, the ever-growing cadre of unmarried teenage mothers.

> Where did they come from, all these educated, accomplished, respectable—and desperately lonely people? Read and weep: they are the casualties of a pointless and destructive, but too long unresisted, war between the sexes.

After all, they are not homeless, nor unemployed, nor on the public dole; eventually, desperate enough, they may even find one another. But they are in their way no less serious a symptom of a social dislocation. The famous young people of yore are, to be sure, now advancing inexorably toward early middle age, and are, for the most part, now also engaged in getting and spending—with, you might almost say, a vengeance. But it is not for nothing that one of the country's better-selling publications is a magazine called, simply, "Self," nor that odd and exotic psychotherapies abound, nor that the country is positively awash in that new psychic solvent called Prozac.

There are other loud detonations on this battlefield I could tell you about, such as the way the world's newest venereal disease, AIDS, has been culturally transmuted into a positively honorific achievement. I don't know if any of you watched the Academy Awards last month, but for those of you who didn't it might be of some interest to hear how Tom Hanks, winner of an Oscar for his performance of a man dying of AIDS in the movie *Philadelphia,* gave his acceptance speech with tears in his eyes and sent greetings to all the "angels in heaven," men who had reached that happy place by virtue of having, unlike Hanks, actually died of AIDS. But to speak of this bewildering development in full detail would require me among other things to describe for you the so-called AIDS-education materials now making their way through America's public schools courtesy of such expert advisors as the Gay Men's Health Crisis—materials whose text and particularly whose graphic illustrations I was loath to show even to my husband. And if not to him, I am certainly not going to make them graphic for you. I need hardly say that the Gay Men's Health Crisis is a government-funded consultant to the educational establishment. AIDS, then, has not only become the occasion for much high sentiment—particularly in Hollywood (the source of so much elevated sentiment in our culture)—but perhaps even more astonishingly, this curse from which there is no reprieve has somehow been turned into an opportunity to instruct the nation's elementary-school children in how to become adept at the very practices—including, I am afraid, anal intercourse—that, aside from the sheer horror of this assault on their childhood—I am talking fifth grade!—would most put them in danger of contracting the disease. I kid you not about what is going on in a number of school systems—the seduction of babies!—nor, take my word for it, am I in the least exaggerating. On the contrary, history will look back in utter mystification at how the carriers of a murderous plague came to be called angels in heaven and were invited to teach the children about health and safety.

In short, as Bill Bennett's *Index of Leading Cultural Indicators* has made so plain, we are in the soup. And I haven't even mentioned the universities—the greatest consumer fraud worked upon a complaisant public since the great South Sea Bubble of the 18th century. Were I to get started on this subject, we would be here until our closing banquet. It is enough to say that everything I have described above has come together in one grand synthesis on the nation's campuses, lustily presided over by those now-tenured former youths of the 1960s.

But blessedly—for me, for you, and for this mixed-up country of ours—the story does not end there. It is true that we all of us have had a hand, if only by default, in this three-decades'-long descent into moral and spiritual tumult; still, we do happily have other claims to make for ourselves. Despite all the moaning and groaning that continues apace in the press and media, for example, the country remains a veritable miracle of productivity—and we have had a hand in this, too. Now, productivity does not come from nowhere; it is an outcome of that other, everyday culture, the one that would have been so much fun to talk about. Moreover, despite all the stress and strain that have been put on our political institutions, they have nevertheless been left standing, a little shaky perhaps, but still in place—and again, we have had a major hand in their survival.

We are free people. Which means: our difficulty is also our possibility.

Mere survival, of course, is not enough. For if it has taken many centuries to create the institutions of a democratic republic like ours, it need surely not take as long to destroy them. After all, to build is a slow process, but to tear down is all too quick and easy. A few sticks of dynamite will do the trick. The engine of our way of life, then, does not come with a lifetime warranty. We are called upon to keep it in repair, not every year or with each quadrennial election, but every single day. If so much of America's public culture has under our not sufficiently watchful eyes become unworthy of the society we have been blessed with the opportunity to live in, we are nevertheless not helplessly in its grip. We are free people. Which means: our difficulty is also our possibility.

The truth is that culturally speaking, we have not sufficiently been standing up for ourselves. This must seem a strange thing to say at a gathering of The Heritage Foundation, an institution which every day battles, and battles effectively—more effectively, indeed, than any other of its kind the world has ever seen—against the legislative and executive and judicial rot. Let me stop for just a minute to say something personal, something I have never said in public before. When I was invited to serve as a Trustee of Heritage—it is by now a goodly number of years ago—I was of course flattered, honored, and also, I may say, amused. Amused, because I was then one of those odd creatures they called a neoconservative, and it made me smile to see the look of intense watchfulness, even suspicion, on the faces of many of my new conservative colleagues: "What manner of being is this?" said the look they gave me, and "What is she really up to?" Ed Feulner, however, was obviously not among them. Probably he knew that I was not going to remain a "neo" anything for long. In any case, he invited me, and I accepted with the keenest pleasure. That pleasure was nothing to the humble gratitude I have come to feel since, for the sheer thrill of being permitted to take part in so vital and winning and forward-looking an enterprise. In a life of fighting many fights against what has been happening, I have had no other comradeship remotely like it. I thank you all. Especially, of course, Ed.

But there is something more, something desperately important, for me and for all of us to engage ourselves in, because Heritage's battles are, and in the nature of things can only be, the public ones. In the way it conducts these battles the Foundation puts strength and hope into us, but it cannot issue *Memoranda* and *Backgrounders* to our hearts or come full blown into our homes and individual lives: I mean the commonplace lives we lead with our friends and neighbors and especially with our children and grandchildren—the lives beyond politics. Here we all of us have our own work to do—work, moreover, that we must carry on mainly by example, above all, by exemplifying the joy that is to be found in leading productive and ordinary lives. These are the lives on which America depends—its real culture.

As for that other culture, the one I was assigned to talk to you about, growing like some noxious weed all over the surface of things, we have to stand ourselves firmly and unswervingly up against it—and keep on standing and never let up. This is not easy: how often have we been made to seem retrograde and tiresome, even sometimes in our own eyes? How often have we been called bad names, been defamed, or worst of all, ridiculed? How often have we seen our deepest beliefs being traduced as we open our morning papers or turn on our televisions or wander into a movie theater? How often have we been made to feel positively homicidal in conversation with our children's teachers or even listening to sermons in our churches and synagogues? What Heritage has to do requires every ounce of its energy, and what we have to do will require every ounce of ours—and then some. Still, we must never forget how privileged we are. For each time we resist some new cultural fashion, we are engaged in nothing less than saving lives. What greater pleasure than that?

> For each time we resist some new cultural fashion, we are engaged in nothing less than saving lives.

And there is another consolation. We alleged fuddy-duddies are actually guests at the very best party, with the liveliest and most interesting company, in town. While the liberal culture is urging its devotees to move themselves permanently into a kind of massive sick room, we get to stay on the outside, urging them instead to come dance and sing and worship and serve and live and produce and be fruitful and multiply out here with us.

Let us admit it. We are having a wonderful time. And admitting it, let us show it and carry along with us all those blessed new generations, those lovely little babies like the one that I saw here this morning and their lovely babies after them. And let us always remember that to be an American is a gift not an entitlement. We are every day given the chance to turn this gift into a priceless treasure. This time, let's not muff that chance.

—Midge Decter spoke on April 15, 1994,
at The Heritage Foundation's Annual Board Meeting
and Public Policy Seminar in Amelia Island, Florida.

11 | The Madness of the American Family

The idea of talking about the subject called "family" always puts me in mind of a line from the ancient Greek playwright, Euripides. "Whom the Gods would destroy," he said, "they first make mad." Now, to be sure, there are no gods—there is only God—and even if there were, you would have to think that, far from destroying us, they are, on the contrary, busily arranging things very nicely for us. Nor do I think that American society has gone mad, exactly. Look around you, at this room, this magnificent city, the magnificent country that surrounds it: You would have to say that somebody is surely doing *something* right. Nevertheless, the ghost of that ancient Greek keeps whispering his words of ageless experience in my ear. If we Americans cannot be said to have gone mad, we have certainly been getting more unhinged by the day.

For instance, we are healthier than people have ever been in all of human history. Just to list the possibly debilitating diseases that American children need never again experience—measles, whooping cough, diphtheria, smallpox, scarlet fever, polio—is to understand why we have begun to confront the issue of how to provide proper amenities to the fast-growing number of people who are being blessed with a vigorous old age. And yet, as it seems, from morning until night we think of nothing but our health and all the potential threats to it. We measure and count and think about everything we put into our mouths. While we are speculating about which of the many beautiful places there will be for us to retire to, we are at the same time obsessed with all the substances and foodstuffs that are lying in wait to kill us, and try out each new magical prescription for the diet that will keep us ever young and beautiful. This has gone so far that, for example, not long ago a group of pediatricians had to issue a warning to new mothers that, far from beneficial, a low-fat diet was in fact quite injurious to infants and toddlers.

> People just like you and me nowadays find themselves... debating about the family: Is it good for you? Is it necessary, especially for children? And— craziest of all— what is it?

And as if an obsession with nutrition were not enough, every day millions upon millions of us whom life has seen fit to save from hard labor find ourselves instead, like so many blinded horses of olden times, daily enchained to our treadmills.

So we treat our health as if it were a disease and the benign conditions of our lives as if they were so many obstacles to our well-being.

And if that is unhinged, what shall we say about finding ourselves engaged in discussing something called the family? How on earth, if the gods are not out to destroy us, have we got ourselves into *this* fix? Talking about the family should be like talking about the earth itself: interesting to observe in all its various details—after all, what else are many if not most great novels about?—but hardly up for debate. And yet people just like you and me nowadays find themselves doing precisely that, debating about the family: Is it good for you? Is it necessary, especially for children? And—craziest of all—what is it?

In our everyday private lives, of course, we drive around in, or fly around in, and otherwise make household use of the products of various technologies of a complexity that is positively mind-boggling without giving it a second thought. Yet at the same time, millions among us who have attended, or who now attend, universities find it useful to take formal courses in something called "family relations," as if this were a subject requiring the most expert kind of technical training. And in our lives as a national community we call conferences, engage in public programs, create new organizations, and beyond that publish and read several libraries of books devoted entirely to questions about the family (not to speak of the fact that here I am as well this evening, offering you some further conversation on the subject).

I look around this room and wonder, how on earth have we come to this place, you and I? How did the wealthiest, healthiest, and luckiest people who have ever lived get to such a point? It is as if, in payment for our good fortune, we had been struck by some kind of slow-acting but in the long run lethal plague. This plague is a malady we must diagnose and put a name to if we are ever as a nation to return to our God-given senses.

Where did the idea that the family might somehow be an object of debate and choice come from? It is never easy, as epidemiologists will tell you, to trace the exact origin of a plague. Who exactly is our Typhoid Mary?

I can't say I know, precisely, but I knew we were in trouble back in the late 1950s when I picked up *Esquire* magazine one day and read an essay about his generation written by a young man still in university which concluded with the impassioned assertion that if he thought he might end up some day like his own father, working hard every day to make a nice home for the wife and kids, he would slit his throat. *Slit his throat.* Those were his exact words.

> **W**here did the idea that the family might somehow be an object of debate and choice come from?

Now, I might not have paid close attention to the sentiment expressed by this obviously spoiled and objectionable brat were it not for two things: First, we were in those days hearing a lot from their teachers about just how brilliant and marvelous was the new generation of students in the universities, and second, *Esquire* was in those days known for its claim to have its finger on the cultural pulse. Thus, this was a young man whose mountainous ingratitude was worth paying a little attention to. And sure enough, not too much later, what we know as the '60s began to happen. Enough said. Should it, then, have come as a surprise that in short order that young author's female counterparts began in their own way to declare that throat-cutting would be the proper response to the prospect of ending up like their mothers? Well, surprise or no, the plague was now upon us for fair.

Am I trying to suggest that the only course of social health is to live exactly as one's parents did? Of course not. The United States is a country whose character and achievements have depended precisely on people's striking out for new territories—actual territories and territories of the mind as well. We have not lived as our parents did, and we do not expect our children—or, anyway, our grandchildren—to live as we do.

Several years ago I was privileged to attend my grandfather's hundredth birthday party. When we asked him what, looking back, was the most important thing that had ever happened to him, without a moment's hesitation he astonished

The young men began to cut out—cut out of responsibility, cut out of service to their country, and cut out of the terms of everyday, ordinary life.

us by answering that the most important thing that ever happened to him was being privileged to witness the introduction of the use of electricity into people's homes. And now I see my own grandchildren, even the youngest of them, sitting hunched over their keyboards, fingers flying, communing with unseen new-found friends in far-flung places and giving this new possibility not a second thought. So of course we do not live as our parents lived, but that young man writing in *Esquire* was saying something else: Underneath the posturing, he was saying that he did not wish ever to become a husband and father. And the raging young women who came along soon after him were saying they, for their part, would be all too happy to be getting along without him.

And what, finally, when the dust of all these newfound declarations of independence began to settle, was the result of this new turmoil? The young men began to cut out—cut out of responsibility, cut out of service to their country, and cut out of the terms of everyday, ordinary life. They said they were against something they called "the system." But what, in the end, did they mean by that? Insofar as the system was represented by business and professional life, most of them after a brief fling as make-believe outcasts cut back into *that* aspect of the system very nicely; but insofar as it meant accepting the terms of ordinary daily life, building and supporting a home and family, they may no longer have been prepared to slit their throats, but they would for a long time prove to be at best pretty skittish about this last act of becoming grown men.

> Underlying the real ideology of the women's movement, sometimes couched in softer language and sometimes in uglier, is the proposition that the differences between men and women are merely culturally imposed—culturally imposed, moreover, for nefarious purposes.

And their girlfriends and lovers? They, on their side, were falling under the influence of a movement that was equating marriage and motherhood with chattel slavery. "We want," said Gloria Steinem, one of this movement's most celebrated spokeswomen ("a saint" is what *Newsweek* magazine once called her), "to be the husbands we used to marry."

Let us ponder that remark for a moment: "We want to be the husbands we used to marry." Underlying the real ideology of the women's movement, sometimes couched in softer language and sometimes in uglier, is the proposition that the differences between men and women are merely culturally imposed—culturally imposed, moreover, for nefarious purposes. That single proposition underlies what claims to be no more than the movement's demands for equal treatment, and it constitutes the gravamen of the teaching of women's studies in all our universities.

And need I say that it has been consequential throughout our society? I don't, I think, have to go through the whole litany of the women's complaints. Nor do I have to go into detail about their huge political success in convincing the powers that be that they represented half the country's population, and thus obtaining many truly disruptive legislative remedies for their would-be sorrows.

Among the remedies that follow from the proposition that the differences between men and women are merely culturally imposed has been that of letting women in on the strong-man action: Why, it was successfully argued, should they not be firemen, policemen, coal miners, sports announcers, or—in many ways most significant of all—combat soldiers? At the outset of the Gulf War, early in that first phase of it called Desert Shield, the *New York Post* carried on its front page a newsphoto—it may have appeared in many papers, or at least it should have—illustrating a story about the departure for Saudi Arabia of a group of reservists. The picture was of a young woman in full military regalia, including helmet, planting a farewell kiss on the brow of an infant at most three months old being held in the arms of its father. The photo spoke volumes about where this society has allowed itself to get dragged to and was in its way as obscene as anything that has appeared in that cesspool known as *Hustler* magazine. It should have been framed and placed on the desk of the President, the Secretary of Defense, the Chairman of the Joint Chiefs, and every liberal Senator in the United States Congress.

That photo was not about the achievement of women's equality; it was about the madness that has overtaken all too many American families. For the household in which—let's use the social scientists' pompous term for it—"the sexual differentiation of roles" has grown so blurry that you can't tell the soldier from the baby-tender without a scorecard is a place of profound disorder. No wonder we are a country with a low birthrate and a high divorce rate.

We see milder forms of this disorder all over the place, especially in cases where young mothers have decreed that mothers and fathers are to be indistinguishable as to their—my favorite word—"roles." Again, you cannot tell—or rather, you are not supposed to be able to tell—the mommy from the daddy. The child, of course, knows who is what. No baby or little kid who is hungry or frightened or hurting ever calls for his daddy in the middle of the night. He might *get* his daddy, but it is unlikely that that would have been his desire. Everybody has always known such things: What is a husband; what is a wife? What is a mother; what is a father? How have we come to the place where they are open for debate?

It is not all that remarkable, for instance, that there should have been the kind of women's movement that sprang up among us. There have from time to time, throughout recorded history, been little explosions of radicalism, of refusal to accept the limits of human existence, and what could be a more radical idea than that there is no natural difference between the sexes? Just to say the words is to recognize that what we have here is a rebellion not against a government or a society, but against the very constitution of our beings, we men and women.

The question is, what caused such an idea to reverberate as it did among two generations of the most fortunate women who ever lived? As for their men, what idea lay at the bottom of their response to all this we do not quite know, for they giggled nervously and for the most part remained silent. But it is not difficult to see that if the movement's ideas represented an assault on the age-old definition of their manhood, it also relieved them of a great burden of responsibility: Seeing that their services as protectors and defenders and breadwinners had been declared no longer essential, they were now free—in some cases literally, in some cases merely emotionally—to duck out for fair.

What could be a more radical idea than that there is no natural difference between the sexes?

And since the condition of families depends to a considerable degree on the condition of marriages, small wonder that the subject of family has been put up for debate. Most recently, we are being asked to consider whether two lesbians or two male homosexuals should not also be recognized as a family. Oftentimes the ostensible issue centers on money; that is, spousal benefits for one's homosexual mate. But actually, as we know, what is being demanded is about far more than money. Money is easy to think about; that's why the homosexual-rights movement has placed such emphasis on this particular legislative campaign. But what is really being sought is that society should confer upon homosexual unions the same legitimacy as has always been conferred upon heterosexual ones.

What comes next, of course, is the legal adoption of children. Why not a family with two daddies? After all, some unfortunates among us don't even have one. (Lesbians, of course, suffer no such complications. All their babies require for a daddy is a syringe. Thus, we have that little classic of children's literature, to be found in the libraries of the nation's public schools, entitled *Heather Has Two Mommies*.)

In other words, when it comes to families, any arrangement is to be considered as good as any other. People don't pick their professions that way; they don't decide where to live that way; they don't furnish their lives or their houses that way; they don't even dress themselves that way. . .but families? Why not? Aren't they, after all, no more than the result of voluntary agreements between two private individuals? And anyway, don't people have rights? Who are their fellow citizens to tell them how to live and decide that one thing is good and another is bad?

The question is, how did we as a society ever come to this disordered place? For one thing, what has encouraged us to imagine that anything is possible if we merely will it to be? And for another, how have we strayed this far from the wisdom so painfully earned by all those who came before us and prepared the earth to receive us? I ask these questions in no polemical spirit, because few of us have not in one way or another been touched by them, if not in our own households, then in the lives of some of those near and dear to us. What is it, in short, that so many Americans have forgotten, or have never learned, about the nature of human existence?

One thing they have forgotten—or perhaps never learned—is that you can't fool Mother Nature. If you try to do so, you sicken and die, spiritually speaking—like those little painted turtles that used to be a tourist novelty for children and, because their shells were covered in paint, could never live beyond a few days. Well, we do not, like those novelty turtles, literally die. On the contrary, as I have said, we have been granted the possibility of adding years to our lives; but far too many of us, especially the young people among us, live what are at bottom unnatural lives. Too many young women, having recovered from their seizure of believing that they were required to become Masters of the Universe, cannot find men to marry them, while the men on their side cannot seem to find women to marry. Both grope around, first bewildered and then made sour by what is happening to them. And there is nothing in the culture around them—that so badly unhinged culture—to offer medicine for their distemper.

Together, marriage and parenthood are the rock on which human existence stands.

What is it Mother Nature knows that so many of us no longer do? It is that marriage and family are not a choice like, say, deciding where to go and whom to befriend and how to make a living. Together, marriage and parenthood are the rock on which human existence stands.

Different societies may organize their families differently—or so, at least, the anthropologists used to take great pleasure in telling us (I myself have my doubts)—and they may have this or that kinship system or live beneath this or that kind of roof. But consider: In societies, whether primitive or advanced, that have no doubt about how to define the word "family," every child is born to two people, one of his own sex and one of the other, to whom his life is as important as their own and who undertake to instruct him in the ways of the world around him.

Consider this again for a moment: *Every child is born to two people, one of his own sex and one of the other, to whom his life is as important as their own and who undertake to instruct him in the ways of the world around him.* Can you name the social reformer who could dream of a better arrangement than that?

Are there, then, no violations of this arrangement? Among the nature-driven families I am talking about are there no cruel fathers or selfish and uncaring mothers? Of course there are. I have said that family is a rock, not the Garden of Eden; and a rock, as we know, can sometimes be a far from comfortable place to be. Off the coast of San Francisco there used to be a prison they called "the rock," and that is not inapt imagery for some families I can think of.

But even in benign families there are, of course, stresses and strains. To cite only one example, it takes a long time, if not forever, for, say, a late-blooming child, or a child troubled or troublesome in some other way, to live down his past with his own family, even should he become the world's greatest living brain surgeon. Families are always, and often quite unforgivingly, the people who Knew You When. So, as I said, the rock of family can sometimes have a pretty scratchy surface. But there is one thing that living on a rock does for you: It keeps you out of the swamps. The most dangerous of these swamps is a place of limitless and willfully defined individual freedom.

The land of limitless freedom, as so many among us are now beginning to discover, turns out to be nothing other than the deep muck and mire of Self. And there is no place more airless, more sunk in black boredom, than the land of

Self, and no place more difficult to be extricated from. How many among us these days are stuck there, seeking for phony excitements and emotions, flailing their way from therapy to therapy, from pounding pillows to primal screaming to ingesting drugs to God knows what else, changing their faces and bodies, following the dictates first of this guru and then of that, and all the while sinking deeper and deeper into a depressing feeling of disconnection they cannot give a name to?

The only escape from the swamp of Self is the instinctual and lifelong engagement in the fate of others. Now, busying oneself with politics or charity—both of which are immensely worthy communal undertakings involving the needs and desires of others—cannot provide the escape I am talking about. For both, however outwardly directed, are voluntary. The kind of engagement I mean is the involuntary discovery that there are lives that mean as much to you as your own, and in some cases—I am referring, of course, to your children and their children and their children after them—there are lives that mean more to you than your own. In short, the discovery that comes with being an essential member of a family.

> The land of limitless freedom, as so many among us are now beginning to discover, turns out to be nothing other than the deep muck and mire of Self.

I do not think it is an exaggeration to use the word "discovery." No matter how ardently a young man and woman believe they wish to spend their lives with one another, and no matter how enthusiastically they greet the knowledge that they are to have a baby, they do not undertake either of these things in full knowledge of the commitment they are undertaking. They nod gravely at the words "for richer or poorer, in sickness and in health," but they do not know—not really, not deep down—that they are embarked upon a long, long and sometimes arduous and even unpleasant journey.

> A woman holding her first-born in her arms, for instance, is someone who for the first time can truly understand her own mother and the meaning of the fact that she herself had been given life.

I think this may be truer of women than of men. A woman holding her first-born in her arms, for instance, is someone who for the first time can truly understand her own mother and the meaning of the fact that she herself had been given life. This is not necessarily an easy experience, especially if her relations with her mother have been in some way painful to her; but even if they have not, this simple recognition can sometimes be quite overwhelming. That, in my opinion, is why so many first-time mothers become temporarily unbalanced.

I cannot, of course, speak for the inner life of such a woman's husband; his experience is bound to be a different one. But the panic that so often and so famously overtakes a first-time expectant father is surely related to it. To become a family is to lose some part of one's private existence and to be joined in what was so brilliantly called "the great chain of being."

In short, being the member of a family does not make you happy; it makes you *human.*

All this should be a very simple matter; God knows, it's been going on long enough. So why have we fallen into such a state of confusion? The answer, I think, lies in the question. By which I mean that we Americans living in the second half of the 20th century are living as none others have lived before. Even the poor among us enjoy amenities that were once not available to kings. We live with the expectation that the babies born to us will survive. The death of an infant or a child is an unbearable experience. Yet go visit a colonial graveyard and read the gravestones: Our forefathers upon this land lived with the experience, year after year after year, of burying an infant—lived two weeks, lived four months, lived a year. How many burials did it take to be granted a surviving offspring? I am not speaking of prehistoric times, but of two hundred years ago. Two hundred years, my friends, is but a blink of history's eye. Could any of us survive such an experience? I doubt it.

Even a hundred years ago—*half* a blink of history's eye—people lived with kinds of hardship only rarely known among us now. Read the letters of the Victorians (fortunately for our instruction in life, people used to write a lot of letters; those who come after us, with our phone calls and e-mail, will know so little about us). They were sick *all the time.* Or take a more pleasant example, provided by my husband, the music nut: We can sit down in the comfort of home every afternoon and listen to works of music their own composers may never have heard performed and that not so long ago people would travel across Europe to hear a single performance of.

So we live as no others who came before us were privileged to do. We live with the bounties of the universe that have been unlocked by the scientists and engineers and then put to use by those old swashbucklers with names like Carnegie and Edison and Ford—and, yes, Gates—who were seeking their own fortunes and in the process made ours as well. Moreover, not long from now, we are told, there will be nearly one million Americans one hundred years old or more. We live, too—and should not permit ourselves to forget it—with another kind of bounty: We are the heirs of a political system that, despite a number of threatened losses of poise and balance, has remained the most benign and just, and even the most stable, in the world.

> The truth is that precisely because we are living under an endless shower of goodies, we are as a people having a profoundly difficult time staying in touch with the sources of our being.

The truth is that precisely because we are living under an endless shower of goodies, we are as a people having a profoundly difficult time staying in touch with the sources of our being. That is why so many young women were so easily hoodwinked into believing that marriage and motherhood were what they liked to call an "option," just one choice among many. That is why so many young men were so easily convinced to settle for the sudden attack of distemper afflicting the women whom fate intended for them. That is why so many people of good will find it difficult to argue with the idea that homosexual mating is no different from their own—everybody to his own taste, and who's to say, especially when it comes to sex, that anything is truer, or better, or more natural than anything else?

In short, because God has permitted us to unlock so many secrets of His universe, we are in constant danger of fancying that any limits upon us are purely arbitrary and we have the power to lift them. In the past half-century, what has not been tried out, by at least some group or other in our midst, in the way of belief and ritual or—horrible word—lifestyle? We have watched the unfolding of catalogues-full of ancient and newly made-up superstitions, the spread of fad medicines and "designer" drugs (each year, it seems, produces a new one of these). Lately we have seen beautiful young children, children living in the most advanced civilization on earth, painfully and hideously mutilating their bodies in the name, they will tell you, of fashion. All this, I believe, stems from the same profound muddle that has left us, as a society, groping for a definition of the word "family." Maybe people are just not constituted to be able to live with the ease and wealth and health that have been granted to us.

But this would be a terrible thing to have to believe, and I do not believe it, and neither do you, or you would not be here this evening. As Albert Einstein once said, the Lord God can be subtle, but He is not malicious. What does seem to be a fair proposition, however, is that given the whole preceding history of mankind, to live as we do takes more than a bit of getting used to. It takes, indeed, some serious spiritual discipline.

I believe that two things will help us to be restored from our current madness. The first is for us, as a people and a culture, to recapture our respect for the wisdom of our forebears. That wisdom was earned in suffering and trial; we throw it away—and many of us *have* thrown it away—at their and our very great peril. The second is a strong and unending dose of gratitude: the kind of gratitude that people ought to feel for the experience of living in freedom; the kind of gratitude the mother of a newborn feels as she counts the fingers and toes of the tiny creature who has been handed to her; the kind of gratitude we feel when someone we care about has passed through some danger; the kind of gratitude we experience as we walk out into the sunshine of a beautiful day, which is in fact none other than gratitude for the gift of being alive.

All around us these days, especially and most fatefully among the young women in our midst, there are signs of a surrender to nature and the common sense that goes with it. The famous anthropologist Margaret Mead—a woman who in her own time managed to do quite a good deal of damage to the national ethos—did once say something very wise and prophetic. She said that the real crimp in a woman's plans for the future came not from the cries but from the smiles of her baby. How many young women lawyers and executives have been surprised to discover, first, that they could not bear to remain childless, and second, that they actually preferred hanging around with their babies to preparing a brief or attending a high-level meeting? One could weep for the difficulty they had in discovering the true longings of their hearts. Next—who knows—they may even begin to discover that having a real husband and being a real wife in return may help to wash away all that bogus posturing rage that has been making them so miserable to themselves and others.

When that happens, we may be through debating and discussing and defining and redefining the term "family" and begin to relearn the very, very old lesson that life has limits and that only by escaping Self and becoming part of the onrushing tide of generations can we ordinary humans give our lives their intended full meaning. We have been endowed by our Creator not only with unalienable rights but with the knowledge that is etched into our very bones.

All we have to do is listen. And say thank you. And pray.

—Published in Policy Review, *September-October 1998.*
Also published as "Family" by The Heritage Foundation.
Midge Decter gave this lecture in Denver, Colorado,
on July 9, 1998, as part of The Heritage Foundation
25th Anniversary Leadership for America Lectures.

12 | Again, The American Family: Lighten Up

Oh, Lord. Imagine having to talk about the family–again. *Families* would be fun; that's just stories about people. But *the* family? Oh, dear. One of the symptoms of just how very abstract is our present-day relation to something called "the family" is that there is no longer any good humor or simple laughter connected with it. How long has it been, for instance, since you last heard a mother-in-law joke? Or even a brother-in-law joke? How can a group of people that includes members of both sexes and at least two generations–indeed, sometimes three generations, and sometimes even four–how can such a group of people manage to live closely together over a long period of time without poking at least a little fun at one another–even if it must be out of earshot?

It's hard to say exactly when the assault on the family which has brought us to this discussion began, but of one thing we can be sure: it began among people who had lost their sense of humor. Men, for instance, used to make fun of women, but now they can practically go to jail for it. Women used to make fun of men, but now they sue them instead. And children? Refer to them within earshot of one's neighbors as "the little brats" and one is liable to be faced with a visit from the authorities.

How long do you suppose human beings can stand this kind of solemnity? No wonder so many men and women nowadays show signs of wishing simply to flee from one another.

The book that might just be the greatest novel ever written, namely, Tolstoy's *Anna Karenina,* begins with the following sentence: "Happy families are all alike; every unhappy family is unhappy in its own way." In our time, alas, we have acquired a great deal of expertise on the subject of unhappy families—indeed, much too much. So for a couple of minutes, before we get down to business, let's just talk about happy ones—or at least not unhappy ones.

> What is properly called a family begins when some man marries some woman and they begin to try to figure out how in God's name they are going to live together peaceably under the same roof.

What is properly called a family begins when some man marries some woman and they begin to try to figure out how in God's name they are going to live together peaceably under the same roof. And sometimes, as we know, at first that is no mean feat. Men and women are after all not constituted the same. They have different wants and needs, and so sometimes, perfectly naturally, they have difficulty understanding one another. About some things, perhaps, they never really do. And under the right circumstances, there is really nothing wrong with that fact. It's just the way things are.

Now, with your permission I would like to pause here for a minute and tell you a strange story about my great grandmother, who lived out her life in an age when the terms of family life were as taken for granted as the weather. She lived, moreover, at the center of a household that down through the years remained a veritable beehive of lively and fun-loving children (my father's side of the family; definitely not my mother's), a beehive of children, grandchildren, great grandchildren, friends and neighbors, and neighbors' children. And she was there in the middle. All of this crowd loved her, depended on her, and doted on her. Not bad. I'd certainly say "happy." Yet when she lay dying, to their utter astonishment she begged her children not to let her husband of more than sixty-five years, my great grandfather, into the room with her. She not only didn't want to speak to him, she didn't want to have to *look* at him. God alone knows what the old man had done to her—whatever it was, it was done in private and was probably something very subtle. For he was in fact a nice old guy. The point of this story is, as Mr. Dooley said about politics, this family stuff ain't bean-bag.

That little old lady, my great grandmother, had no choice but to live as she did. And you would have to say that even though at the end she wanted no part of her husband, she was a woman well-rewarded for the way she lived. The question, then, is, what is it in our world of ever-advancing modernity, this world that afflicts people with the sense of seemingly endless choice, what is it that makes happy families all alike—as Tolstoy, who knew everything, said? It seems to me there are four things that hold a man and a woman—and hence a family—together: One is the need for shelter, for the comfort of a place to retreat to in a not always benign world. The second thing is the need for companionship that one can count on without having to go through hoops. The third—maybe for some it is the first—is the love of children. And the fourth is the need to be forgiven for one's all too human weaknesses. (This last, of course, is where the humor comes in.) Indeed, all of these things together is what they mean when in that old-time ceremony they say, "for better or for worse." Even only three out of the four reasons for getting married that I listed would make, if not a perfect, at least a not bad, example of what Tolstoy meant by happy families.

So what has been going wrong? Why do we nowadays stand around at each wedding ceremony wondering if, or for how long, this is going to last? (Please note that for the purposes of this discussion, I am not speaking about the famously troubled and troubling non-family life of the inner city: all those children without fathers and sometimes practically without mothers as well. That problem has its own separate origins and its own special character, and to discuss it here seems to me to be just a way for us to get ourselves off the hook of discussing the difficulties that nowadays beset so many of us and our own sons and daughters.)

Well, I am not a cultural historian. (Nor, to my everlasting sorrow, am I Leo Tolstoy.) So you won't hear some grand cultural-historical theory from me. But I do feel safe in saying that among all the troublesome developments of the past half-century, none has bit so deeply into the flesh of the family as the Women's Liberation movement. Talk about humorless! Now, most people, especially men, have to this day refused to confront the real meaning and message of this movement. They have preferred instead to comfort themselves with the idea that the women's movement was merely intended to be a means of overcoming certain age-old inequities in women's education and employment. You know: the old "equal pay for equal work." That makes it a matter of justice; and we're all for justice, aren't we. But, of course, the women's movement has never been anything of the sort. In recent years, as we are beginning to see, the movement seems to have moved largely off-stage—even Gloria Steinem is now happily married—but it has done its damage and left behind a wide swath of wreckage, intellectual as well as social wreckage.

For underneath all the talk of fairness what this movement was really saying was this: "For thousands of years it has been hateful to be a woman, and now we are going to get our own back and make it as hateful as possible to be a man." Does this sound crude? A caricature? I recommend that one day you go to the library, take out a book called *Sisterhood is Powerful,* and read it—you men especially. (Even that long ago movement for women's suffrage, by the way, was not just out to redress a true injustice and pass the 19th Amendment that gave women the vote. One of its slogans was "Votes for women; chastity for men.") But for the purposes of our discussion today, let's take Women's Lib at its mildest, by which I mean its most—albeit grudgingly—accepting of marriage and the family as an institution that was not going to go away.

But first, I would like to tell you about, a document that was published in 1971 in a magazine called *Ms.* and that was subsequently widely quoted and reprinted in movement publications. This document is a marriage contract, drawn up by a woman named Alex Cates. This is not the kind of model agreement between husband and wife that would have to do with "in sickness or in health, till death do us part" or anything like that, but one that outlines in day by day, minute by minute, detail just which household and family roles will be performed by mommy and which by daddy on which day of the week. For instance, she does home laundry and he does dry cleaning delivery and pickup. She prepares dinner on Monday, Wednesday, and Friday, and he, on Tuesday, Thursday, and Saturday. (And how they manage on Sunday you wouldn't want to know.) The one who invites guests must see to the preparation of food for them and must clean up after. This contract goes so far as to assign the nights of the week on which the father is to answer the children's questions or comfort them should they wake up crying. And there is more—but you get the idea. The point is not how many of the contracts were actually drawn up and signed, but rather the popularity of this document among the more moderate members of Women's Lib as an ideal of marital relations. And do not fool yourselves. From the movement proper this ideal was spread far and wide, from the universities to the press to the pulpit to the sitcoms. Think of it: no please, no thank you, no offering help to one another and no gratitude for favors received—an image of married life that could send an icy chill down your spine, and that did cast an icy pall over many a new marriage.

Let me read you in full one passage of the contract that is the true chiller and that far more than the silly assignment of domestic tasks sums up both the tone and the attitude that has seeped beneath the flooring of millions of American households. Listen carefully. This passage says: *"We reject the notion that the work which brings in more money is more valuable. The ability to earn more money is a privilege which must not be compounded by enabling the larger earner to buy out of his duties and put the burden on the partner who earns less or on another person hired from the outside."* Translate that into plain talk, and it means that regardless of the fact that he may work long hours to support his wife and children in fine style—do not forget from which class in this society the membership of the women's movement came—no special consideration will be due him—and no gratitude either. Since that time, of course, many young wives have gone into law firms or to Wall Street and become serious breadwinners. Are we to suppose that as far as the women's movement is concerned, the fact that they now may be earning a lot of money will not allow them to get out of their share of the housework by "putting the burden on another person from the outside"? No, that passage in the contract was directed at husbands only and was intended to let them know that from now on their being breadwinners didn't count for anything.

And how did men, one of whose major contributions to their families as well as sources of self-respect was to keep a roof over the heads of their wives and children—how did they respond to the idea that doing this was of no special value? Well, some—in fact many—simply took a powder, some became dandies, some became clinically depressed, some became *un*-clinically depressed, some spent long hours in the gym working on their abs and pecs and working out their aggressions, and some surrendered and, adding contempt to their wives' movement-inspired hostility toward them, *did* the dishes on Tuesday, Thursday, and Saturday, *took* and collected the dry cleaning, and dried their children's nighttime tears on the nights specified—and wondered why the little lady was *still* not satisfied.

> Marriage and the family are institutions answering primarily to the needs of women and invented for their benefit. It is in their nature to be monogamous, and to need protection and defense and support for themselves and their children.

All this I think is looking up these days. At least some of the young women are staying home from the law firms and banks nowadays to look after the babies they discovered, just under the wire, that they wanted to mother. Perhaps—who knows?—should they need help around the house, they might even ask their husbands nicely for it.

But even so, something about marriage and family remains a terrible secret in this so very enlightened time— the old truth, you might say, that dare not speak its name. And that is, that marriage and the family are institutions answering primarily to the needs of women and invented for their benefit. It is in *their* nature to be monogamous, and to need protection and defense and support for themselves and their children. In exchange, they agree to supply men with the comforts of home, the comforts I spoke of earlier: a place to be oneself, to hide from the pressures of the world outside, some easy companionship, children with which to claim the future, and forgiveness for weakness. It's actually, when you think of it, a pretty good deal all around. But only if you do two things: one, accept its terms, and two, lighten up.

As a mark of how bad we allowed things to become, we now have a movement dedicated specifically to strengthening the traditional family. As it happens, I know many of the leaders of that movement. I honor and respect them. And I do hope that one day they will remember to include among their ambitions the restoration of at least some of the old inescapable comedy of men and women, separately and together.

−Midge Decter spoke at The Heritage Foundation's Leadership Conference and Board of Trustees Meeting in Dallas, Texas, on April 6, 2001.

13 | Losing the First Battle, Winning the War

S trange as it probably seems, in the week when all Americans are abuzz with the election—some abuzz with hope and some, of course, with nervous anxiety—I don't want to talk about the election. Rather, I would like to begin by taking you back to a certain truly dark and dangerous hour in 20th century history: the last week of May in the year 1940.

The German army is advancing through France like a knife through butter; in only a few days the Swastika will be flying over Paris. The Allied troops, primarily British, with a group of Belgians and Frenchmen who have refused to surrender thrown in, have been pushed back to the coast of the British Channel and are gathering, huddling really, along the waterfront of a French harbor town called Dunkirk. The British Admiralty decrees they must be taken out of there immediately, and to aid in this job presses everyone in England who owns a private boat, no matter how small, into joining with the British Navy on the rescue mission. The participation of small boats turns out to be providential, because by the time the British expedition reaches Dunkirk, German bombardments have killed thousands of British troops and put the port out of commission. Thus the men have to be ferried out to the ships by British fishermen and Sunday sailors who are able to navigate close to the shore and take the men off the beach. It takes something like a week to complete this operation, and, in all, 198,000 British and 140,000 French and Belgian troops were saved to fight another day.

Now, say what you admiringly will about the famous stiffness of the old British upper lip or shake your heads if you will in wonderment at the sheer grit involved in the operation of getting all those men out of what would otherwise have been a massive German deathtrap; the truth is, Dunkirk represented a vast and terrible Allied defeat. This defeat was, you might say, a special gift to Western Europe from a group of British men of so-called "reasonableness" and "good sense," who during the preceding decades had prided themselves on being political realists (we have such men ever with us, it seems). These were the men who had two years earlier cheered the outcome of the journey of the British Prime Minister, Mr. Neville Chamberlain, to a place called Munich, where, boasting of "peace in our time," he managed among other things to hurl the Czechs into close to 50 years of ugly occupation, first by the Nazis and then by the Communists.

As it happened, only two weeks before Dunkirk, the men of so-called practical reason had at long last lost the confidence of the British nation, and the Prime Ministership was handed by his failed and demoralized predecessor to a member of the cabinet named Winston Churchill. This Churchill, as we all happily know, set about to carry his nation with him in what turned out to be the salvation not only of Britain but—it is no exaggeration to say—of no less than Western civilization itself.

The reason I have presumed to remind you of something many of you here today know every bit as well as I is that few things provide so perfect an example of what I want to discuss than the story of Britain in May of 1940. It would, of course, take a year and a half and the near destruction of the U.S. Navy in Pearl Harbor—another bitter defeat—before the United States was to join the war. Meanwhile, this little island off the coast of Europe, having taken a terrible pasting in the air war known as the Battle of Britain, managed by spirit alone, as it were, to induce the Germans to aim their sights elsewhere.

Now most people would agree—certainly most of the British at the time would have agreed—that by himself Winston Churchill had a great deal, if not everything, to do with lifting the hearts and stiffening the spines of his countrymen. On the eve of a new administration in Washington it seems to me especially interesting to inquire just how he managed to do that. Did he say to the people "When this war is over, I'm going to guarantee you all free medical care"? Or did he say, "When this is over, I'm going to begin regulating those famous 'dark, satanic mills' that have so famously been polluting our beautiful midlands"? Or did he say, "When this is over, I am going to assure all you pensioners a clean and fresh new flat and a worry-free old age"?

Do I have to remind you of the answer? What he said was: "I have nothing to offer you but blood, toil, tears, and sweat."

Now, we have just lived through one of the less inspiring presidential campaigns in living memory, in which we were invited to witness debates and seemingly endless campaign patter about such things as the cost of prescription drugs and only a couple of small and barely audible quibbles about how the United States should comport itself in an eternally turbulent world.

When in the last half-century do you remember that anything truly difficult was seriously asked of us as citizens?

But I ask you just for a moment to set aside what might be a somewhat spoiled celebration, if celebration it should turn out to be, and consider the following question: What might have happened if someone running for office in the United States at some time in the recent past had stood up before the American public and said, "I have nothing to offer you but toil and sweat"—blood and tears being for the moment not particularly relevant—"I have nothing to offer you but toil and sweat, virtue, honor, and in the end, national greatness"? Do you suppose he might forthwith have been simply ridiculed or perhaps slapped into a straitjacket? Well, possibly, but let me tell you what I think would have happened: I think the whole damn country would have stood up and cheered.

Year in and year out we have been promised much, and now and then—for instance, 20 years ago—many of the things we hoped to hear were said, some even delivered. But when in the last half-century do you remember that anything truly difficult was seriously asked of us as citizens?

In Vietnam, for example, we suffered more than 50,000 casualties, and yet Lyndon Johnson, the man who sent half a million men there to fight, was heard more than once to express his satisfaction with the way he had never, as he called it, "stirred up war fever"—meaning, he had never sought the full-hearted support of the public by explaining what we were doing in that war and why it was important to us. Then, for the sake of a little social peace, Richard Nixon went him one better by cutting our boys loose from ever being pressed into service, and thereby also cut them loose from the idea that they might owe something for the comfort and ease and safety of the world around them.

Ronald Reagan, who at least believed in the better angels of our nature, spent eight years cheering our hearts and straightening a few flabby spines on the subject of the Soviet Union versus democracy, but even he in the end demanded almost nothing of us.

Instead, this is how it has been for nearly 40 years now: Angry women have continued to storm the halls of government declaring that their already unimaginably privileged lives must be freed of any and all remaining traces of difficulty, while a lot of insulted and angry men for their part took this as an excuse to begin ducking out on what used to be considered their hallowed obligation. Angry black officials have by means of a whole variety of gestures insistently demanded of the government something that could only be provided by themselves. Meanwhile the schools have largely given up on the task of educating, and colleges have been surrendering their once-honored franchise to every passing anti-intellectualism. And everywhere we have turned, we have been almost unrelievedly showered with smut, on television, on the Internet, in bookstores, in the movies, on the magazine stands, where even what were once called "ladies' magazines," purveyors of fashion and recipes, now feature advice in every issue on how to achieve for both oneself and others a heightened sexual satisfaction. We are so bombarded with stimulae to prurience that most of us have reached a point where we barely notice any more.

> We require our politicians to promise that they will do for us all kinds of things that we must, and can only, do for ourselves.

And in general, any hope of our bringing some clean, fresh air into such vital areas as the relations between the races, as well as those between the sexes, as well as into our classrooms, and into our public culture, any such hope day by day falls under the sway of our sloth. Instead, we require our politicians to promise that they will do for us all kinds of things that we must, and can only, do for ourselves.

Take one example that has lately become very popular among politicians, the schools. Our schools, no question about it, need to be forced to straighten up and devote themselves to teaching our children again. But let's be honest: what role beyond articulating his views can the President really play in such an effort? Start a new department, fund new research, or for the hundredth time add his prestige to some new gimmick or program? And how long have such forms of presidential action already been taken—and with what results?

We have been saying for years that something must be done about the persistent use of drugs among the nation's kids, to use another example. But what is it that the President or the political system is supposed to do? Pass another law, or better yet, pay some third-world government to send its army after the growers? And what do *we* do in the meanwhile? Resolve to find a way to protect our children from themselves or demand action from anyone and everyone so long as it is not us?

Then there is the issue of the low and brutish quality of public entertainment, particularly those forms of it that are so eagerly consumed by our children. Again, ask yourselves with full honesty what useful power a president—or any other politician—is actually able to exercise with respect to this problem. Is he the one mandated to keep watch over our children? While we do what? Demand that everything threatening to their well-being be made by the authorities to go away?

The truth is, we tend to wait for someone else, someone high up—call him Mr. President or Mr. Speaker or Mr. Justice—to fulfill responsibilities that are, and must be, primarily our own. We ask the men we elect to fight with the schools in our stead, to turn our children away from drugs in our stead, and, in general, to clean up our culture in our stead. Pass a law, we demand, or finance a new program, or sometimes perhaps just offer some consolation and sympathy.

What, we ask, can we be expected to do about all this. After all, the culture is so strong and our children will be so unhappy with us if we attempt to keep them from its blandishments.

I am certain that it is precisely our will to have others do our work for us—not only assure the condition of our bodies but also the condition of our spirits—that leaves so many of our fellow citizens complaining of an inexplicable feeling of boredom, and, beyond boredom, of some indefinable and untreatable case of the blues.

"I have nothing to offer you but blood, toil, tears, and sweat," said the man to a people suffering the first murderous sorrows of what was to be a long and murderous war, a people—and here is the point—who as a nation would never again in history be so gallant and high of spirit as they were when they opened themselves to this stern call.

Now we, too, are at this moment in a kind of war—not a bloody war, of course, not a war that will smash our houses and swell our graveyards, but in its own way decisive: a war of minds and spirits to determine whether a people as unimaginably wealthy—wealthy beyond the dreams of potentates of old—as vigorously long-lived, and as blessed by fortune as the American people can sustain a decent national life.

At the dedication of the Civil War graveyard at Gettysburg, as any schoolchild ought to be able to tell you but probably can't, Mr. Lincoln spoke of our nation as one "conceived in liberty and dedicated to the proposition that all men are created equal" and the war over which he presided was a test to determine whether, in his words, "any nation so conceived and so dedicated can long endure." He did not, as we know, live to see the ultimate outcome of that test, but we certainly have. Indeed, it is we who are its most privileged beneficiaries: citizens as we now are of the oldest continuous democratic government in the history of the world. Just think about that for a minute: the oldest continuous democratic government in the whole history of the world.

In our national political life, surely we shall not soon, if ever again, look upon the likes of President Abraham Lincoln—among other extraordinary things, one of the greatest of American writers. Nor shall we look upon the likes of Mr. Jefferson Davis either—a gentleman to put the hubbub and gracelessness of our current-day political transactions forever to shame. But what our Founding Fathers cobbled together—and perhaps they themselves would be surprised to discover—turned out to be a work of political architecture that has been able to withstand just about every kind of human foible and limitedness and treachery. There have not been, for instance, very many genuinely great men occupying the White House, nor are there likely to be many in the future. Genuinely great men, you might say, do not grow on trees. But the system does not require genuinely great men—that is its genius.

> What our Founding Fathers cobbled together—and perhaps they themselves would be surprised to discover—turned out to be a work of political architecture that has been able to withstand just about every kind of human foible and limitedness and treachery.

What the system does require, however, is a responsible citizenry. In this system, the politicians are to be advised and led by us, not the other way around. (It seems funny even to be speaking such a sentence in the presence of a group like you, the closest friends of the Heritage Foundation—for that, of course, is precisely what Heritage is and has ever been about.) What usually happens instead, however, is that the politicians do not so much listen to us as pander to the lowest of our lower natures.

Imagine telling people who think nothing of spending untold thousands of dollars on vacations and entertainment—I live in New York City, for example, when at Christmas time one can hardly venture into the streets for the crowds—telling people who think nothing of eating in expensive restaurants and paying $80 for a theater ticket that they deserve to be given free medication. Imagine the politicians talking with a catch in their throat about society's injustices to the elderly. (I realized not long ago with a considerable shock that that meant me.) Imagine the politicians talking that way as if this were, say, the 19th century, when honesty requires the recognition that the elderly in this blessed, blessed country have on average a good deal more wealth than their offspring.

So the politicians, even the best of them, appeal to our baser instincts, in the belief that it is a sanctioned professional necessity for them to do so. And, alas, I guess we have given them a good deal of cause to believe it because we are busy people, because we sometimes feel timid, and because, in the comfort of our unbelievably comfortable lives, we often grow slothful.

But how many of us did not stand up and cheer, for instance, when a man named Ward Connerly took it upon himself, virtually all alone, to set off a campaign against that ugly piece of social engineering called affirmative action. Or when a man named Ron Unz practically by himself successfully overturned in the State of California that too-long established injustice to children called bilingual education. Or when our own Bill Bennett stood before the board of Time Warner and caused them all, especially their particularly smug chairman, to grow pale simply by reading the lyrics of a particularly vicious rap song distributed by Warner Brothers Records and challenging them with the simple question, "What kind of people are you?"

As I said, we are in our own kind of war. There is no blood to shed, as there was for those whose monuments we are about to visit and who did so much—who in some sense did everything—to preserve for us our own good fortune. But if there is no blood to shed, there is sweat and there is toil, and with no single monumental figure like Mr. Churchill to hold us to the job, we, all of us, are on our own, together.

> Precisely in our good fortune, it is time for us—all of us—to take upon ourselves the work of recovering what has been lost—in other words, to become the kind of citizens upon which the Founding Fathers once believed the American system would ultimately have to stand.

Last week, I was in Budapest and learned something very important from those Hungarians. They live in a small country, still recovering from what the Communists did to them, and they have bitter internal political squabbles and say terrible things about one another, the Left about the Right and the Right about the Left. But they have something in common that to this day keeps their spirits enviably high, which is the communal memory of their revolution against the Communists in 1956. They were, of course, too weak to stand against the superior force of the Red Army and its tanks for long, but stand they did until they could stand no longer, and because of that, in a very moving way, they remain a people full of pride and hope, whoever their political leaders.

We not only have no Churchill to speak to us majestically of the toil ahead, we, unlike the Hungarians, have no oppressors to help us stiffen our spines. But precisely in our good fortune, it is time for us—all of us—to take upon *ourselves* the work of recovering what has been lost—in other words, to become the kind of citizens upon which the Founding Fathers once believed the American system would ultimately have to stand. Only then will we have the teachers and schools and artists and entertainers and, yes, the political leaders that we all so deeply wish and deserve.

This task is not one for a President, whoever he may be. Nor is it one for Congress, whatever its composition. The work I am talking about is the work of citizens—it is *our* work. *We* must lead *them*. Not merely by voting, but every day, with our voices, our shoulders, and our continuing determination, each and every one of us.

It is grueling and, yes, sometimes dirty work, the work of preserving and protecting and defending this blessed system, a system of which we are the uniquely privileged heirs. Toil, tears, and sweat are as necessary as they ever were. So I say, no time is better than now, and no one more appropriate than we ourselves. As we gather here at this meeting, for the time being without a President-elect, let us dedicate ourselves to fulfilling our own part in directing the future of this great enterprise.

Man the little boats! There are still hundreds of thousands—indeed, millions—in need of rescue.

—Midge Decter spoke at a meeting
of The Heritage Foundation's President's Club on
November 10, 2000, in Washington, D.C.

14 | Learning to Live with "Yes"

C an anyone here have forgotten, even to this day, the pure air of euphoria that hung over Ronald Reagan's first election and inauguration?

And how about when the Berlin Wall came down and all those prisoners of the Warsaw Pact began streaming toward freedom?

And after that, the collapse of the Soviet Union itself. Those, too, were times of euphoria, a public happiness some of us had thought we would never in our lifetime be able to experience. Though Reagan was no longer in office, both we and the Eastern Europeans knew that the world owed these happy times, in very large measure, to him.

After all, such moments, such feelings, are seldom if ever afforded anyone who pays serious attention to the political life of this nation. So, I must beg your pardon during this final gathering of this most pleasant meeting. (Indeed, it always seems my fate to do so among my friends at Heritage.) I must beg your pardon because I mean to speak to you about some things that are rather less euphoric than our memories of Ronald Reagan.

Take November 2000. That certainly wasn't a cheery time. After all, we came as close as a hair to losing that election. Remember? And won it, when we did, by a means that should have made us all extremely uncomfortable.

I am referring to victory in an election by means of a decision of the Supreme Court, a bad and, who knows, possibly very dangerous precedent.

At best our response to the Supreme Court's decision on the outcome of that election ought to have been nothing more cheerful than an enormous sigh of relief.

I know full well, of course, that it was we who were in danger then, in danger of having the election stolen from us outright before our very eyes. We sat in front of our televisions and with growing rage watched the entirely visible and shameless televised manipulation of those ridiculous Florida voting cards, not to mention the bitter comedy provided by that group of either genuinely or perjuriously feeble-minded ladies (I haven't made up my mind which) from West Palm Beach, who claimed en masse to have made mistakes in marking their votes. Still, at best our response to the Supreme Court's decision on the outcome of that election ought to have been nothing more cheerful than an enormous sigh of relief.

Nor was there much pleasure for us to be found of that famous map of the United States with its red and blue voting populations. To be sure, certain Republicans of my acquaintance found it in their hearts to gloat over the fact that their man had so visibly commanded the loyalty of the great American heartland.

But in truth, there should have been nothing to give any of us, indeed of either party, much happiness in that red and blue image in a country with so stark a cultural split as that map testified to.

Remembering it somehow reminds me of a story told in one of the chapters of a marvelous book called *Founding Brothers* by an immensely gifted and quite mysteriously self-destructive historian named Joseph Ellis.

The story is of two delegations of Quakers, one from New York, one from Philadelphia, who in February of 1790 presented petitions to the then brand new House of Representatives. These petitions called for the infant federal government to put an immediate end to the African slave trade.

Now, at the Constitutional Convention in Philadelphia, Congress had specifically been prohibited from passing any law that abolished or restricted the slave trade before the year 1808, that is, 18 years into the future.

Thus the Southern representatives were in a fury with the petitioners. For several of these Southerners had only recently been at the convention in Philadelphia and could testify to the fact that absent a guarantee not to put an end to the slave trade until 1808, the Constitution would never have been approved in the first place, nor would it subsequently have been ratified by several of the Southern states.

The Southerners understood full well that tampering with the date of the slave trade would inexorably lead, and indeed was intended to lead, to a battle over the abolition of slavery itself.

But, as Mr. Ellis tells us, James Madison, himself a Southerner, of course, did not want to face the issue head-on, and sought instead for a way to fudge it. That seems to have been one of Madison's great skills. He wanted to fudge by allowing the petitioners to present their documents to the House and then forwarding them on to—what else?—a committee to study them.

That way, Madison believed, the issue would more or less evaporate with the passage of time. But things did not quite work out as Madison had hoped, because on the very next day, yet another such petition, this one from a group known as the Pennsylvania Abolition Society, was presented to the House. This document arrived with the endorsement of Benjamin Franklin himself, next to George Washington, be it remembered, possibly the most admired figure in the country at that time.

Thus, though the petitions were indeed forwarded to a committee where, as Madison had hoped, they lapsed into at least temporary obscurity, the truth was that all too dangerously early in its existence, the House had come within a hair of being embroiled in a deadly constitutional crisis.

This crisis, as we know, would continue to bubble and would ultimately boil over some 70 years later. Nor would it really cool down in men's hearts until something like 100 years after that.

Were those delegations from Philadelphia in the right, morally speaking? I think none of us can really deny that they were. The slave trade was, after all, an unmitigated human horror. But the defense of it mounted so angrily on that occasion by the Southern representatives did not in fact have to do with morality at all.

Slavery had been instituted in the South long before the creation of the United States. By 1790, it had become essential for the economic survival of the region, as its economy was then constituted. But the Southern planters were very different from, and were engaged in an almost wholly different enterprise from, that of those hardy and independent New England brahmins, economically dependent as these planters were on a system that combined large holdings of land with the cheapest of labor.

> Our government, it gives me not a second's pause to say, is both the most benign and the most stable on the face of the earth.

It seems to me, then, that though they presented an unanswerable and moving moral argument, the anti-slavery petitioners of 1790 were in the wrong, including even, I must say, in the moral wrong, because had they succeeded in their effort to have the House ban the slave traffic, they would thereby also have succeeded in destroying that then so new and so brilliantly conceived and so very hard-won government, which is, I need hardly remind you, our government still—the government, it gives me not a second's pause to say, that is both the most benign and the most stable on the face of the earth.

Had those petitioners succeeded, the country's map, so far from being divided into two colors, might to the unimaginable sorrow of everyone in this room, have turned out to be a veritable rainbow, a rainbow of empires and monarchies and ways of living, and above all, a land inhabited by a variety of hostile peoples vying for its riches.

So, grateful that the United States did in fact hold together to become a great nation (and it is well now and then to remind ourselves after how much cost in blood and suffering and treasure), I ask you now to return to the matter of November 2000's nevertheless disquieting division into blue and red. For at that moment, it seems to me, none of us doubted that those colors bespoke what was a political and cultural reality on the ground.

> **Grateful that the United States did in fact hold together to become a great nation, it is well now and then to remind ourselves after how much cost in blood and suffering and treasure.**

Boston, New York, and southward some of the way long the East Coast, and let us not forget those two great Yuppie havens, Vermont and New Hampshire, all this was Al Gore country, as on the opposite coast was Seattle to Portland to San Francisco and—how could we forget?—on to Hollywood.

If you will forgive me for a personal aside, I can't help mentioning that perpetual exception to any kind of rule about American politics that is plunked right in the country's upper middle, my own birthplace, the ever unaccountable great State of Minnesota, sometimes red, sometimes blue, sometimes green, purple, or God knows what, at present boasting a deep-dyed Socialist Senator and an equally deep-dyed wacko—I am not prepared to say precisely what kind of wacko—of a Governor.

In any case, this visible division of the country seemed like no joke. True, electoral politics can sometime provoke a laugh or maybe a ticklish shudder or two. After all, people can only vote for one of the choices they are presented with. These choices are in turn presented to them by local political parties that can themselves sometimes be jokes. I offer in evidence of this proposition the present day Republican Party of the great State of New York.

But if election choices can now and then be not all that serious, the ideas by which people live always are. Whether they are conscious ideas or so deep below consciousness as to remain instinctive, ideas are the forces that govern human lives and that sometimes govern deaths as well.

Ironically, it is the liberals who are out to conserve what they have established in this society and it is we conservatives who are out to bring change.

I would venture to say that it was our sense of the conflict of ideas, rather than of parties merely, that accounted for how intently we recognized and responded to that visible manifestation of the division of November 2000.

We understood that the arrangement of those two blocks of colors was nothing more than a pictorial representation of the ever-ongoing battle between what we call liberal ideas and what we call conservative ideas. The reason I am so tentative in these designations is that right now, ironically, it is the liberals who are out to conserve what they have established in this society and it is we conservatives who are out to bring change.

In that red heartland, many of us declared, is the society where what we call "traditional values" live. On the country's two shores, east and west, are to be found the societies where our so badly corrupted, greedy and heedless and downright dangerous high culture lives and breathes.

Thus, at least to some of us, it looked like war. That war, that culture war we had spoken of so often had now been oh, so neatly imprinted across the very geography of the United States of America. Now, as I said, when we talk of the war of ideas, what we mean by this is not merely a Democrat versus Republican dispute about the level of taxation, say, or who should be responsible and how responsible they should be for the retirement of the health care of the country's youngest and oldest citizens. Such disputes, important as their outcomes may be, are in truth only the outward manifestations of the real war that is being waged, which is—I don't know how else to say it—a spiritual one.

The fundamental idea of liberalism on which its political programs are all based, as well as its notions of how, for example, to go about shaping the minds of the country's children, the fundamental idea of liberalism is that societies determine all the conditions under which its members either prosper or suffer.

Thus, a truly good society would owe it to every member of the population that he be well and benignly provided for by his government. To the extent that a society falls short of this accomplishment, it must be mobilized, legislatively and bureaucratically, to make up whatever the shortfall should turn out to be, whether moral, physical, or social.

Whereas the fundamental idea of conservatism is that the members of a good society will, within necessary bounds, be assured their individual freedom and will, as a defining condition of that freedom, assume full moral and social responsibility for themselves and their children, these two views of society in their pure form are basically irreconcilable. The politicians representing them may and do arrive at compromises with one another. Many of the problems they attempt to deal with probably do not in any case cut as deep as this suggests. But when it comes to the questions that cut to the very bone of human existence—to name but a few, sex, marriage, birth, death, family obligations, self-discipline, work, faith, charity—when it comes to these there is no committee, such as James Madison might have devised, to keep them from creating conflict.

Things were not always this way, of course, in the United States of America. However badly behaved Americans could be toward one another—and they were, whites toward blacks, old families toward the newly rich, the native born toward immigrants, and so on—everyone, rich or poor, Western, Eastern, Northern, Southern, was agreed on such fundamentals as what a father was and what he was supposed to do and what a mother was and was supposed to do and what a family was and was supposed to do, what was guilt and what was innocence, what was Godly and what was ungodly.

The fundamental idea of conservatism is that the members of a good society will, within necessary bounds, be assured their individual freedom and will, as a defining condition of that freedom, assume full moral and social responsibility for themselves and their children.

They did not necessarily live up to what was required of them, these Americans, but there was little doubt among them about what constituted a decent life. At some point, as we know, this ceased to be the case. Everything from God on down or from conception on up came to be considered a suitable matter for fundamental debate.

> **Everything from God on down or from conception on up came to be considered a suitable matter for fundamental debate.**

That is precisely why the map of November 2000 was so disquieting, not because Al Gore almost became President. Bad as it would have been, this country has survived worse. In addition to Mr. Gore's boss, may I name Jimmy Carter?

No, as the man once said, there is a lot of ruin in a nation, especially in a nation as strong and storm weathered as this one. We were disquieted in November 2000 because it looked to the eye fixed on that map that the country was poised on a knifepoint. 2000, in other words, was the emotional exact opposite of 1980. We heaved a sigh of political relief, true, a condition very far from euphoria. At the same time, we experienced a pang of cultural anxiety.

Well, my friends, have no fear. If you think I'm going to leave you here in late 2000 consoled for your election anxiety at least to some extent by the not yet faded hope of such good things as lower taxes and better elementary schools, if you think that, then let me most cheerfully assure you, you are mistaken.

For what had seemed to be suggested by that map of red and blue, that is, a society engaged in outright cultural war, less than a year later turned out instead to have been merely a society in a state of frozen and slothful uncertainty.

This uncertainty was not the malaise that Jimmy Carter had once so foolishly charged his fellow Americans with, but rather the result of the spiritual weariness that had overtaken millions of people who could no longer figure out just what their society needed of them.

Ronald Reagan had asked them to become that great shining alabaster city on a hill and their hearts had been lifted up. They responded with enthusiasm, because given the choice people prefer greatness to its opposite.

Reagan's opponents, of course, never understood this. They thought he was popular just because he talked so good, not because of what he said, which is precisely why they could never really lay a glove on him. But alas, Reagan's successors, so far from urging greatness upon their fellow Americans, in effect invited them to rest their spirits once more.

The first of these successors took them into a war, which he then for some mysterious reason decided not to win, and leaving the job undone, blamed them for his decision to do so. The second of these successors, Mr. Clinton, while forgetting his own private peccadilloes, which is admittedly difficult to do, there was also that halfhearted and contradictory and sometimes downright incomprehensible mess that passed for his foreign policy.

Thus it was that in the year 2000, George W. Bush inherited a public, millions upon millions of whom had for 12 long years been receiving a message from the White House that they were merely people whose votes were exchangeable only in the currency of government perks and benefits.

> People were reminded of how to be citizens. Maybe more importantly, they were reminded of how to be fellow citizens.

Now, admittedly perks and benefits are hard to resist. But they hardly add to anyone's citizenly morale, not to mention anyone's feeling of strength and self-reliance.

Then came September 11th, 2001. In addition to everything else you might say about that terrible day, and I sometimes think we are in danger of talking ourselves into a state of sentimental anesthesia about it, whatever else you might say about September 11th and the war it has led us into, it certainly separated the blue sheep from the red goats.

People were reminded of how to be citizens. Maybe more importantly, they were reminded of how to be fellow citizens. I can tell you that beyond being moved and overwhelmed and grateful, we New Yorkers were somewhat astonished by the outpouring of care and concern for us coming from places and people in this country, people who, on the basis of the way they used to talk, we had always assumed harbored hostile feelings toward us.

Whenever something really bad would happen in New York, for instance, my own Minnesotan mother would sigh with a certain pleasure and say, "Well, we don't have that in our part of the country."

It is, of course, because he released the longing of so many previously demoralized Americans once again to become serious and responsible citizens that Mr. Bush continues to enjoy his through-the-roof popularity.

I do not mean to suggest that those bi-coastal areas and particularly the colleges and university campuses all across the nation that are really part of their territory, I don't mean to suggest that they have been completely transformed, that they have turned from blue to red.

For our political as well as cultural health, we had best recognize that the cultural hard core, that mélange of black and feminist and gay extortionists, reflexive anti-capitalists, sexual libertarians, village atheists, and so on will never go away. Some number of them will be there on those coasts, peddling their wares on the stage and screen and air and in the press and, as I said, on campus, probably forever. (But who knows, maybe only forever as old folks reckon time.)

Nevertheless, we now have a new kind of opportunity to beat them back as an influence on public policy. You have to remember, though it's sometimes hard to do so, that all the praise and prizes and awards and tenured promotions and sinecures that the blue people are constantly being showered with are actually only the praise, prizes, awards, and sinecures they bestow on one another. Exposing them to the heat of strong and good argument both confuses and weakens them, as nowadays does the popularity of George Bush, along with the whole war against terror.

The question from those journalists that poor Don Rumsfeld is forced to listen to day after day—"Is Osama bin Laden dead or alive?"—the question asked plaintively as if the answer alone will constitute the ultimate judgment of American success or failure, is vivid evidence of precisely the current feeling of weakness on the part of those who are doing the asking.

> A victorious America is nowadays a country that protects its people by conducting warfare, hot or cold, as the situation dictates and for however long it takes; warfare against the forces that threaten decent democratic society.

In truth, knowing no more of their country's history than Vietnam and of Vietnam itself knowing almost nothing, many of the journalists have not yet made up their minds as to which way lie those Pulitzer Prizes, whether through cheering for American victory or looking forward to American defeat.

But that newly energized part of the American public that is now saying an energetic "yes" to their President, they know which way lies what they prize. It lies in being the passionate citizens of a victorious America. A victorious America is nowadays a country that protects its people by conducting warfare, hot or cold, as the situation dictates and for however long it takes; warfare against the forces that threaten decent democratic society.

In saying "yes" to their President, in other words, all those members of the American public are saying "yes" to us as well. This "yes" is not perfect from our point of view. It doesn't yet, for instance, carry them to all of the policies we believe in. Nor is this President perfect from our point of view. His signing of that hurtful and crazy Campaign Finance Reform bill, his imposition of the steel tariff, these are things inconsonant with our beliefs and hopes.

For myself, I could also wish that he would apply to that old, seasoned nine-lives terrorist Yasser Arafat the same standard he applies to al-Qaeda, a group which, by the way, Arafat helped to train. But these are matters of policy and we know why the President has given in on them, for the sake of his war.

One could only wish that Lyndon Johnson had tried to bring the country with him in Vietnam, instead of boasting, as he did, that he was prosecuting a war, these were his words, "without stirring up war fever." The world might have been left a better place if he had done a little bit of that kind of stirring.

The President will make mistakes for the sake of his war. We must expect that. War can be a confusing business, churning up conflicting opinions, ambitions, and purposes around the man in charge.

This war, if its purpose is rightly pursued, will be both a long and far from simple one. So we must help the President in whatever way we can to stay the course and call on the people who are with him to remain staunch. He may yet even need to borrow their sons for his war. For if we are not victorious, with or without allies and coalitions, not only we, but the whole wide world will have hell to pay.

We must also expect that a lot of the people now saying "yes" to us are going to need a lot of tender and careful and persistent arguments from us about what might turn out to be a lot of issues.

Once in the bad old days, a friend of mine who had been a 1930s leftie and had quickly seen the light was challenged on some point by a young 1960s radical. My friend turned to him and said, "I would love to argue with you about this, but to tell you the truth, by now I have forgotten the answers."

If we are not victorious, with or without allies and coalitions, not only we, but the whole wide world will have hell to pay.

Well, we are going to have to remember the answers and insist on them for as long as it takes. We conservatives are not very good, or I should say have not usually been very good, at hearing "yeses" that are uncertain or incomplete. But now is the time, if ever a time there was for us to be not only confident, but patient and serene and cheerfully dogged.

This country's future and not this country's alone is in our hands. In that dogged serenity we can turn a still somewhat uncertain "yes" into a positively reverberating clap of thunder. Then, listen as this great country of ours heaves a loud sigh of happiness, a sigh of happiness that will be heard and that will bring new hope to the whole presently demoralized, but surely still yearning world beyond our borders.

We may not be Ronald Reagan's City on a Hill, but holding him in our memory and answering every "yes" with a "yes" of our own, we may at least strengthen the country's muscles for the climb up to it.

—Midge Decter spoke at a meeting of
The Heritage Foundation Board of Trustees
on April 6, 2002, in Dallas, Texas.